REGIONAL SPILLOVER EFFECTS
OF THE IRAQ WAR

W. Andrew Terrill

December 2008

*****

The views expressed in this report are those of the author and do not necessarily reflect the official policy or position of the Department of the Army, the Department of Defense, or the U.S. Government. This report is cleared for public release; distribution is unlimited.

*****

The author would like to thank Mary J. Pelusi, Dr. Phil Williams, Dr. Norman Cigar, Dr. Steven Metz, Dr. Dallas Owens, Dr. Douglas Johnson, and Sarah E. Womer for useful and insightful comments on earlier drafts of this work. All mistakes in this work of fact, omission, interpretation and speculation are, nevertheless, entirely my own.

*****

Comments pertaining to this report are invited and should be forwarded to: Director, Strategic Studies Institute, U.S. Army War College, 122 Forbes Ave, Carlisle, PA 17013-5244.

*****

FOREWORD

The Iraq war has been one of the dominant factors influencing U.S. strategic thinking in the Middle East and globally since 2003. Yet the problems of this highly dynamic and fluid war have sometimes forced U.S. policymakers to address near-term issues that cannot be safely postponed at the expense of long-term strategic thought. Such a technique, while understandable, cannot continue indefinitely as an approach to policy. Long-term planning remains vital for advancing regionwide U.S. and Iraqi interests following a U.S. drawdown from Iraq. Such planning must include dealing with current and potential "spillover" from the Iraq war. In this monograph, Dr. W. Andrew Terrill presents ideas, concerns, and strategies that can help to fill this gap in the literature and enrich the debate on the actual and potential spillover effects of the Iraq war that will face U.S. policymakers, possibly for decades.

Regional spillover problems associated with the Iraq war need to be considered and addressed even in the event of strong future success in building the new Iraq. In less optimistic scenarios, these issues will become even more important. Spillover issues addressed herein include: (1) the flow of refugees and displaced persons from Iraq, (2) cross-border terrorism, (3) the potential intensification of separatism and sectarian discord among Iraq's neighbors, and (4) transnational crime. All of these problems will be exceptionally important in the Middle East in the coming years and perhaps decades, and trends involving these issues will need to be closely monitored. Of these problems, Dr. Terrill clearly is especially concerned with the spread of sectarian divisions which, if not properly managed, can have devastating regional consequences. This monograph, however, forms an important baseline useful for considering future trends in each of the areas that he has identified.

The Strategic Studies Institute is pleased to offer this monograph as a contribution to the national security debate on this important subject as our nation continues to grapple with a variety of problems associated with the U.S. presence in Iraq and the larger Middle East. This analysis should be especially useful to U.S. strategic leaders as they seek to address the complicated interplay of factors related to Middle Eastern security issues and the support of local allies. It may also be useful to those considering how to optimize the U.S. national interest in dealing with nonallied states within the region. This work may also benefit those seeking a greater understanding of long-range issues of Middle Eastern security. We hope this monograph will benefit officers of all services as well as other U.S. Government officials visiting Iraq and its neighbors.

DOUGLAS C. LOVELACE, JR.
Director
Strategic Studies Institute

BIOGRAPHICAL SKETCH OF THE AUTHOR

W. ANDREW TERRILL joined the Strategic Studies Institute (SSI) in October 2001, and is the General Douglas MacArthur Professor of National Security Affairs. Prior to his appointment, he served as a Middle East nonproliferation analyst for the International Assessments Division of the Lawrence Livermore National Laboratory (LLNL). In 1998-99, Dr. Terrill also served as a Visiting Professor at the U.S. Air War College on assignment from LLNL. He is a former faculty member at Old Dominion University in Norfolk, Virginia, and has taught adjunct at a variety of other colleges and universities. He is a retired U.S. Army Reserve lieutenant colonel and Foreign Area Officer (Middle East). Dr. Terrill has published in numerous academic journals on topics including nuclear proliferation, the Iran-Iraq War, Operation DESERT STORM, Middle Eastern chemical weapons, ballistic missile proliferation, terrorism, and commando operations. Since 1994, at U.S. State Department invitation, Dr. Terrill has participated in the Middle Eastern Arms Control and Regional Security (ACRS) Track 2 talks, which are part of the Middle East Peace Process. He also served as a member of the military and security working group of the Baker/Hamilton Iraq Study Group throughout its existence in 2006. Dr. Terrill holds a B.A. from California State Polytechnic University and an M.A. from the University of California, Riverside, both in Political Science. He also holds a Ph.D. in International Relations from Claremont Graduate University, Claremont, California.

SUMMARY

The author examines some of the most significant ongoing transnational or "spillover" problems associated with the continuing conflict in Iraq, with particular attention being paid to those problems that could disrupt or even undermine the stability of regional states beyond Iraq. Spillover issues addressed include: (1) refugees and displaced persons fleeing Iraq in large numbers for neighboring countries, (2) cross-border terrorism, (3) intensification of separatism and sectarian discord among Iraq's neighbors fueled by conflict in Iraq, and (4) transnational crime. This work assumes that spillover influencing neighboring states will continue to occur even in best case scenarios where the Iraqi government rapidly assumes full sovereignty over the entire country in ways that allow it to provide security and stability to most of the population. In the perhaps more likely event that Iraq continues to wrestle with serious internal conflict, cross-border spillover problems could be significantly more intense. This monograph is designed to serve as an overview of the present dangers for Iraq's neighbors and may intensify as a result of the ongoing conflict within Iraq. It assumes that no amount of U.S. effort and resources can compensate for Iraqis who are not willing or able to address the serious problems that still exist in organizing their society in ways that promote stability and minimize internal division. It is important that any future setbacks in the strategic situation in Iraq do not lead to intensified problems in the wider Middle East because U.S. strategists and policymakers focus so directly on short-term Iraqi issues that they fail to address how Iraqi problems influence the wider region. The time to begin dealing with the potential dangers of serious spillover problems is immediately, and not after the United States begins to withdraw from Iraq. The alternative approach, which is to assume that the United States will "fix" Iraq and therefore not have to deal with spillover issues, presupposes an almost perfect long-term outcome to the present situation, and is therefore a considerable gamble. At the present time, the danger of spillover problems involving Sunni-Shi'ite sectarian and Arab-Kurdish ethnic strife that moves beyond Iraq is probably more threatening to U.S. interests than any other spillover effect, including the Iraqi refugee crisis, terrorism, and Iraqi-based transnational crime. All of these issues are nevertheless important, and they must therefore be addressed by a comprehensive strategy.

REGIONAL SPILLOVER EFFECTS
OF THE IRAQ WAR

INTRODUCTION

The Iraq War has raged for over 5 years with future Iraqi stability and effective governance subject to considerable levels of uncertainty despite the recent emergence of tangible positive trends there, including a significant reduction in violence. The impact of this long-standing conflict, as well as the Iraqi attempt to redefine its social and governmental structures in the post-Saddam years, has already gone far beyond the borders of Iraq. Other Middle Eastern states, particularly neighboring countries, have been influenced by conditions and activities in Iraq as well as by Iraqi problems that have now assumed a transnational dimension.

Clearly, Iraqi government leaders are also becoming increasingly impatient to take responsibility for the future of their country, and the prospect that the majority of U.S. forces now in Iraq may be withdrawn within the next few years further alters the internal dynamics of the country.[1] Iraqi leaders will then either succeed or fail in efforts to build a united, stable, and inclusive political entity. If they fail or meet only partial success, dangerous repercussions will be felt throughout the region.

This monograph is designed as an overview of how the ongoing conflict within Iraq has created serious and evolving problems that influence neighboring states in a variety of ways. Some of these states are U.S. allies or other friendly countries. U.S. national interests in the wider Middle East will therefore be influenced as difficulties in Iraq affect them. Spillover-related problems and instability in other, less friendly

1

regional states may also influence U.S. strategic interests, although probably in less tangible ways. This work does not predict either an improvement or a worsening of the long-term security situation in Iraq, but rather seeks to consider current and potential ways in which neighboring states will be affected should the Iraqi government be unable to establish enough control over the country to mitigate the problems underlying the spillover effects discussed throughout this work. Spillover issues that have created ongoing difficulties for neighboring countries and addressed herein include: (1) the flow of refugees and displaced persons from Iraq, (2) cross-border terrorism, (3) the potential intensification of separatism and sectarian discord among Iraq's neighbors, and (4) transnational crime.

The transnational problems listed above could present great danger of intensification during times of transition for Iraq, particularly as the Iraqi government moves to address its internal security concerns with fewer U.S. troops available for combat roles. As suggested earlier, the eventual removal of U.S. combatant forces will almost certainly change the dynamics of the Iraqi internal security situation. Correspondingly, there is ongoing concern over whether Iraq's nascent constitutional institutions can survive a U.S. withdrawal. Conversely, it also remains doubtful that a further lengthy stay by U.S. troops will be acceptable to most Iraqis. In assessing Iraq's chances for a hopeful future, an issue of special importance centers on whether the Iraqi government can establish enough domestic legitimacy to maintain the political and judicial institutions necessary to adjudicate conflicting priorities rather than falling back on mass repression or raising the specter of ethno-sectarian civil war. Indeed, some of the U.S.-led coalition's short-term tactics for improving the Iraqi situation may hold the potential to harm Iraqi national unity if such efforts are not properly managed. These tactics include U.S. support for anti-al-Qaeda Sunni militias (sometimes designated the Awakening (*sahwat*) Councils, or Sons of Iraq).[2] Such groups, while enormously useful in opposing al-Qaeda fighters, may be difficult if not impossible to demobilize peacefully even if noncombatant jobs are made available for their members, since many Sunnis may view demobilization as leaving their communities defenseless against an untrustworthy Shi'ite-dominated government, as well as any residual terrorists.

Another danger is that an Iraq that appears stable when U.S. forces leave that country may find itself on a downward spiral once the U.S. military is no longer present to help suppress inter-Iraqi problems. Ultimately, nothing about the future of Iraq is assured no matter how much non-Iraqi effort and resources are thrown into the battle to save it. In the 1950s and 1960s, France and especially the United Kingdom made a considerable effort to prepare some of their colonies for future independence and self-government. A variety of countries (such as Ghana and Nigeria) appeared well-prepared for independence, but then faced severe problems with civil disorder, human rights violations, partial economic collapse, and repeated military coups once the imperial power had departed.[3] Decolonization did not always turn out this badly, but these examples underscore the limits on a foreign power imposing lasting institutions on another society. Moreover, while the United States is not a colonial power in Iraq, it seeks the same goal as many colonial powers did in the 1950s and 1960s — leaving behind a friendly, viable, and potentially prosperous independent nation. Once the majority of U.S. forces leave Iraq (as they eventually must), the durability of the institutions it has helped to create will face their most serious test. In a failed outcome, whereby full Iraqi domestic security cannot be established, a problematic situation in Iraq cannot be allowed to undermine the internal security of other states within the region in ways that lead to unnecessary humanitarian disasters, heightened terrorism, regionwide instability, and even a series of regional internal wars and insurgencies.

REFUGEE MOVEMENTS RESULTING FROM THE IRAQ CONFLICT

One of the most pressing problems facing both Iraq and its neighbors is the challenge created by the movement of massive numbers of Iraqi refugees. Iraq has produced 4.2 - 4.8 million internal and external refugees since 1991, accounting for almost one-fifth of its population. The majority of these refugees fled as a result of ongoing war, although large numbers of Iraqis also departed earlier as a result of United Nations (UN) sanctions against Iraq and decades of Ba'athist misrule. Currently, over two million Iraqis live outside of their homeland, mostly in neighboring countries. The current Iraq War and the preceeding era of sanctions have correspondingly produced one of the largest movements of refugees in any Middle Eastern conflict since at least the first Arab-Israeli War of 1948-49. The conflict has also produced a significantly larger flow of refugees than occurred during the Vietnam War and its aftermath, and is now regarded as one of the two most challenging refugee crises on the planet (the other being the flight of refugees from Afghanistan).[4]

A number of Iraqis left their country before the present conflict began in 2003, and the numbers then dramatically intensified following the ouster of the Saddam Hussein regime and the subsequent chaos that developed throughout the country, including crime and insurgency.[5] Approximately 2.4 million of Iraqi refugees have fled the country, while the remaining approximately 2 million have become internally displaced in Iraq. Syria and Jordan have accepted the largest number of refugees. Up to 1.4 million displaced Iraqis reside in Syria, with official estimates of 450,000-500,000 in Jordan, although more may be present. Also, around 200,000 Iraqi refugees are in the Arab Gulf states.[6] Sizable numbers of Iraqi citizens have also migrated to Egypt, Lebanon, and Turkey. Perhaps surprisingly, relatively few Iraqis have fled to Iran despite the long border between the two countries. The admittedly very different circumstances of the Iran-Iraq War produced around one million Iraqi refugees who fled to Iran or in some cases were deported by the Iraqi regime as potential subversives during the 1980s.[7] According to the Office of United Nations High Commissioner for Refugees (UNHCR), there are only around 54,000 Iraqi refugees in Iran.[8] Some estimates suggest that around 60 percent of the displaced are children.[9]

The most common reason for Iraqis to have fled to neighboring countries is that remaining in their homes has become unacceptably dangerous for themselves and their families. Many have received either explicit or indirect death threats from armed groups, including sectarian militias and criminal gangs. Sometimes militia members will inform families that they are in danger from "bad elements" and need to move among their "own people" to be safe.[10] In some of the more

5

blatant instances of forced displacement, individuals and families have been given 24 hours to leave their homes or face the strong possibility of being killed after the deadline. Some people also were told to leave and take nothing with them. Often Iraqis victimized in this way have been threatened, evicted, and in some cases killed for no other reason than being a member of the wrong religious sect during a process of sectarian "cleansing."[11] Others are believed to be unsupportive of the local militia, or they simply had homes and material possessions that the groups evicting them wanted. Muqtada al-Sadr's Mahdi Army militia, for example, acquired large numbers of stolen residences and vast amounts of material goods in this fashion.[12]

A less dramatic reason for the refugee flow from Iraq involves the extreme difficulties of making a living there. Unemployment was reported to be around 50 percent in the first few years following the U.S.-led invasion and was severely aggravated by the 2003 U.S.-ordered disbanding of Iraq's 500,000-man army, as well as ongoing de-Ba'athification efforts.[13] Other jobs in the government and oil industry also disappeared in the aftermath of the invasion due to the new Iraqi government's inability to establish its authority throughout the country. By 2006-07, the Central Intelligence Agency's (CIA) unclassified *World Factbook* estimated the Iraqi unemployment rate to be between 18 and 30 percent.[14] More pessimistically, Iraqi Ministry of Labor estimates placed it at between 35 percent and 50 percent in 2008, although both American and Iraqi statisticians face tremendous difficulties in gaining an accurate understanding of the employment situation due to political instability.[15] Currently, Iraqi employment seekers who do not have the right personal connections frequently have to pay bribes to obtain available jobs. Often these bribes are beyond the means of most Iraqis.[16] Sunni Arabs also maintain that they are often discriminated against for government employment due to Shi'ite mistrust of them.[17] Government jobs tend to be the most coveted form of employment in Iraq and still vastly outnumber private sector jobs.[18]

An especially unfortunate aspect of the refugee crisis is that at least 40 percent of Iraq's professional class has fled the country. While unskilled Iraqis fleeing to neighboring countries often have difficulty obtaining work, skilled professionals have a more reasonable chance. Many of the most educated and wealthy Iraqis began to move abroad in the 1990-2003 time frame because of a lack of options in Iraq.[19] This exodus included many of Iraq's secular Shi'ite leaders who felt the double bind of enduring the consequences of UN sanctions and being out of favor with the government.[20] Later, after Saddam's 2003 ouster, Iraq's remaining professionals and their families were often the first victims of violent crime, especially kidnapping for ransom. Many Iraqis who left the country in the 2003-04 time frame were able to do so in a planned departure that allowed them to preserve at least a portion of their assets. Additionally, secular, middle-class Iraqis, who were not likely to affiliate well with local militias, were particularly prone to leave in the aftermath of the 2003 invasion. Later waves of refugees, however, were often composed of more desperate people who usually fled in a haphazard way after being overwhelmed by the collapse of law and order.[21]

The departure of large numbers of Iraq's professionals and middle-class individuals has clearly damaged Iraqi rebuilding efforts and removed many of the people who are most necessary to maintain and consolidate a stable and democratic political system. The loss of professional services has also harmed the lives of ordinary Iraqis who have remained. An example can be seen in the departure of Iraqi physicians, at least a third of whom have fled the country as life became increasingly dangerous and unbearable for them (although a few are now returning).[22] Desperate to deal with this problem, the Iraqi government responded by ordering medical schools to stop issuing degrees to recent graduates temporarily in an effort to render them unemployable as physicians outside Iraq (although there is a thriving black market in forged degrees).[23] The exodus of doctors, nurses, educators, and other important service providers has adverse ripple effects since others have been encouraged to leave by the absence of services provided by such individuals. We should also note that the exodus of wealthy and middle-class Iraqis compounds the already serious shortage in some professional and managerial positions brought on by widespread de-Ba'athification.

Refugee Needs and Problems.

The exodus of large numbers of Iraqi refugees has presented severe challenges to neighboring states called upon to assist and host them. Many Iraqis entered host countries only after substantial portions of their financial resources were exhausted or abandoned in Iraq. These refugees, nevertheless, have ongoing needs for housing, jobs, financial assistance, access to children's education, and medical support, including access to mental health services that can help individuals and especially children with war-related psychological difficulties.[24] Remedial education for Iraqi children is also a pressing need for refugees. In the last decade of the Saddam Hussein regime, many

Iraqi families were forced to remove their children from school for economic reasons associated with the difficulties of living under the sanctions regime and Saddam's distorted spending priorities.[25] After Saddam was toppled, widespread poverty remained, and school attendance was further undermined by the danger of sending children into areas where they could be kidnapped. Upon fleeing from Iraq with their families, many children remained outside of any educational system because of the initial reluctance of some host countries to provide free education for noncitizen students and because of family needs for the children to earn money through work during school hours. A number of Iraqis were also concerned that sending their children to school would create documentation that could enable the host government to locate and deport them. A limited number of Iraqi children were placed in private schools, but this option has only been available to more affluent refugees.

The UN classifies most Iraqi refugees as having "temporary protective status" rather than designating them as permanent refugees due to the official expectation that they will be able to return to Iraq when the fighting abates.[26] This approach dovetails with host country concerns whereby Iraqis are sometimes viewed through the prism of the Palestinian refugee problem. In the Palestinian instance, Arab-Israeli fighting caused many Arab countries to become burdened with a permanent Palestinian refugee presence, which never abated. The Palestinians, however, cannot be deported back to their country of origin, while Iraqis can. Some Iraqi refugees correspondingly fear that they will not be welcomed indefinitely by neighboring states and therefore do not register their status with host governments or even with international organizations such as the UNHCR for fear that calling attention to themselves may lead to possible future deportation or other legal problems. An uncertain number of refugees apply for asylum elsewhere once they have reached Syria or Jordan but seldom find another state that will accept them.

The willingness of Syria and Jordan to continue hosting large numbers of Iraqis is also problematic. While both states have struggled to address the issue, the Syrian and Jordanian economies are not strong and can be further harmed by additional refugee influx. Tensions have also arisen with host country populations due to concerns that refugees overburden services and contribute to inflation.[27] Host governments and international organizations are also concerned that those refugees with few options, little money, and no legal right to work may turn to crime as their only alternative. Many Iraqis are correspondingly interested in immigration to Western countries because they believe that such a move will allow them to find employment and is also the best way to avoid being involuntarily returned to Iraq at some later date.[28] Nevertheless, moving to the West to live is often extremely difficult and expensive. Some Western countries, including the United States and many European Union (EU) countries, accepted only limited numbers of refugees in the early post-Saddam years, but they are now beginning to increase their quotas.[29] Other countries such as Sweden have accepted larger numbers of Iraqis, although even the Swedes are reexamining their liberal immigration policies.[30]

Until recently, the United States has provided only limited direct funding for refugee relief, although significant U.S. funds were provided to some of the nongovernmental organizations that are involved in refugee relief.[31] Additionally, there is at least an implied relationship between the aid granted to Jordan and the support Amman gives to Iraqi refugees. Also, in 2008, the United States implemented an important expansion of the visa program designed to facilitate the entry of "at risk" Iraqis and their families.[32] The Iraqis involved with this program have often been threatened by terrorists and face a serious danger of being murdered for their collaboration with the U.S. Government.[33] Anecdotal information suggests that some of these Iraqis may settle their families in the United States, establish their own permanent residency, and then return to Iraq as contract employees of the U.S. Government. This approach allows them to support efforts to build a new Iraq, while knowing that their families are safe.

At this point, there has been no program to establish a network of long-term refugee camps for the Iraqis in Syria, Jordan, or anywhere else outside of Iraq. A temporary camp that was set up at Rweished, Jordan, in 2003 has now been closed with the aid of the UNHCR.[34] There are also two camps in Syria which house Palestinians who have crossed the border from Iraq.[35] Humanitarian organizations tend to favorably view the effort to help refugees without creating camps as they consider these camps to be an often miserable and dehumanizing last resort for dealing with dis-placed people.[36] Still, serious problems exist. Instead of being placed in camps, Iraqis have usually moved to host country cities and most often the slums of these urban areas. In Syria, where the poorest refugees have often traveled, many Iraqis have flooded into the most impoverished neighborhoods of Damascus and other urban centers. Some of these people receive aid services from international organizations, although this support is usually quite meager. There are also fears that international aid organizations will face problems maintaining even their current limited level of support due to rising global food prices.

Iraq's other refugee problem involves internally displaced people. Refugees within Iraq do not constitute a spillover effect of the current Iraq fighting and consequently are mostly outside of the scope of this analysis. Nevertheless, they do constitute potential transnational refugees in the future and may be among the first to seek shelter abroad in the event of either intensified fighting in Iraq or the rise of a strong government unfriendly to the concerns of the individuals of all major religious sects. Currently, large numbers of internal refugees live in squatter villages with few or no services to meet basic needs such as sanitation, public health, water, power, garbage removal, and education.[37] These people are often poorly educated, without skills, and reluctant to register with the Iraqi government as displaced persons for fear of being placed on an official list which they believe might eventually be used for a variety of unfriendly purposes after their names, sect, and family data are obtained.

Syria and the Iraqi Refugees.

Syria has borne a disproportionately heavy role in addressing the refugee problems by accepting 1.2 - 1.5 million Iraqi refugees.[38] At various times, as many as 20,000 Iraqis per day have crossed the Syrian border in buses and other vehicles, forming lines up to 15 miles long at the crossing point at al-Tanf.[39] Many of these people entered Syria without skills or substantial resources. Professionals and more well-off refugees have usually gone to Jordan, the Gulf, or, in some relatively rare instances, to Europe and Canada. The

Iraqi refugees have added to the burden already created by the presence of more than 400,000 Palestinians in Syria.

The Syrians have expressed strong concern that the refugee problem was placing an intolerable strain on their economy over time despite their best efforts to cope with the crisis. Under unrelenting economic pressure, Damascus closed the border with Iraq in October 2007. Syria did so after claiming that Iraq refugees were costing the government $2 billion per year, and after previously tightening entrance visa requirements since at least February 2007.[40] Prior to the Iraqi refugee crisis, Syria did not usually require visas from travelers from other Arab countries.[41] In a fairly clear criticism of the United States, the Syrians also accused the nations which initiated the Iraq War of doing little to manage the refugee crisis that they helped to create. The poor relations between Syria and the United States naturally complicate coordination on this issue, although some U.S.-Syrian discussions on refugees issues have occurred, and U.S. officials have praised Damascus for its support of the refugees.[42]

The Syrian media has also complained of severe inflation and a significant burden on public services as a result of the influx of Iraqi refugees. The educational infrastructure is especially burdened with problems, including overcrowded classrooms, double shifts for teachers, and the use of other makeshift measures, due to the admission of Iraqis.[43] While such efforts underscore Syria's commitment to help the Iraqis, a large number of Iraqi children are not enrolled in schools of any kind. Part of the reason for this problem is that many refugees have temporary residency permits and therefore have especially good reasons to fear deportation if they draw too much attention to themselves or their families. Syrian hospitals and other health care facilities are also suffering from a lack of resources to meet medical challenges associated with the entrance of large numbers of refugees, including many with health problems.

The Iraqi population displacement into Syria has also produced some security problems which are currently manageable but could become more serious over time. Syrian authorities are consistently concerned that Iraqi refugees in their country will bring sectarian vendettas and radical politics across the border with them. This concern seems justified by the fluctuating and unpredictable levels of sectarian bloodshed in Iraq, although only a few incidents that are causes for Syrian unease have occurred so far. In particular, caches of weapons from Iraq have been seized at homes in Damascus, and former officials of Saddam Hussein's military have been found murdered in Damascus.[44] At present, the scale of this problem is apparently quite low, and the evidence of these problems remains anecdotal.[45] According to the International Crisis Group, brawls and killings among rival Iraqi sectarian groups in Syria "remain marginal but . . . on the rise."[46] Such problems are disturbing to Damascus, and Iraqi sectarianism is an unwelcome import on any scale due to Syria's own diverse population and especially its history of sectarian tensions between the ruling Alawis (sometimes considered a branch of Shi'ite Islam) and the majority Sunnis.[47] Syria also has a Kurdish population of around 2 million and a variety of smaller minority groups. Additionally, the Syrian security establishment has consistently viewed the refugee population as possibly containing spies working for unfriendly nations, jihadi militants hostile to the Syrian government, and political agitators of various stripes.[48]

Also a problem with crime and especially prostitution exists among destitute Iraqi refugees with no other options to support themselves and their families. One account states that "tens of thousands" of women and girls in Syria support themselves in this way.[49] Tragically, Iraq women forced into this life are in danger not only from the normal hazards associated with prostitution but have in some instances been murdered by male relatives in "honor killings."[50] In a number of cases, women have fled Iraq without male relatives because they have either been killed or remain involved in the ongoing fighting there. These women can be especially vulnerable to criminal elements. In another form of criminal activity, the tightening of border security by Iraq's neighbors has led to a significant expansion in the production of fake passports and false identity papers. These are services that are useful for terrorists and transnational criminals as well as illegal immigrants.

Jordan and Iraqi Refugees.

Jordan has fewer refugees than Syria, and a significant segment of Iraq's economic elite and professional class have fled there, as well as many poor people.[51] In the last few years, there has also been an increasing number of impoverished refugees entering Jordan, as well as the development of economic difficulties among once prosperous Iraqis whose resources have been diminished, lost, or used up.[52] Various estimates of up to 1,000,000 refugees in Jordan were made in the mid-2000s, but these approximations are now widely believed to be too high. The rough figure used most often until late 2007 was 750,000.[53] More intensive surveying in 2007 established the figure of between

450,000-500,000 Iraqis living in Jordan, mainly in Amman. This survey that served as the basis for this figure was conducted by Norway's Institute for Applied International Studies under a contract from the Jordanian government.[54] While the survey was sophisticated and used multiple indicators, sampling error resulting from secrecy among the Iraqis seems possible. Many Iraqis in Jordan have currently overstayed their visas, according to the Jordanian Ministry of the Interior, and these people would be particularly unlikely to be open and cooperative with pollsters.[55] Others are working illegally without permits. Many displaced individuals are reluctant to share information about their status or activities with what they might view as any official or semi-official organization. Even those who do not fear deportation understand that they may be fined more than they can easily pay if they have failed to renew their visa and other relevant paperwork on time.

As with Syria, the infusion of refugees comes at an unfortunate time for Jordan. The economy was severely battered following the 2003 invasion of Iraq and the dramatic escalation in oil prices that has steadily followed the beginning of that conflict. Prior to the U.S.-led invasion, oil sold on the world market for around $30 per barrel. The world market price is around $60 per barrel in late 2008 (down from a $147 high). While many other oil importing countries have reeled under the high price of oil, Jordan suffered some especially strong economic shocks since it previously received some of its oil free and the rest subsidized from the Iraqi government under Saddam Hussein.[56] Jordanians have, correspondingly, seen significant increases in the price of food, fuel, and other necessities. Additionally, the influx of Iraqi refugees has sometimes been blamed for aggravating the significant difficulties already influencing the Jordanian economy. Housing has become a particularly serious problem, and the cost of purchasing or renting residential property in Amman has skyrocketed.[57] This change has occurred because of increased demand for housing but also because of widespread real estate speculation spurred by the presence of Iraqis.[58] The degree to which hosting the refugees is contributing to these difficulties is subject to considerable disagreement. A 2007 Centre for Strategic Studies (University of Jordan) analysis concludes Iraqi refugees are not the major cause of inflation; rather the increased price of energy due to the end of Iraqi cheap and free oil is a more significant force pushing inflationary trends.[59]

Like the Syrians, Jordanian officials have some security concerns involving the large number of Iraqi refugees in the country. Some officials fear bloodshed between Sunni and Shi'ite refugees (up to 200,000 Shi'ite refugees are currently in Jordan), but no serious violence between the sects is known to have occurred.[60] Jordan has been widely praised for its willingness to help refugees, but such support cannot be extended indefinitely and without more serious limits on the number of Iraqis allowed to enter the country. A turning point came when Jordanian policies for granting visas became more stringent following the November 2005 terrorist bombings of hotels in Amman.[61] These strikes were carried out by al-Qaeda operatives who entered the country from Iraq and thereby underscored the problems with allowing the wrong people to cross the border. Jordanian authorities are often suspicious of young Iraqi men, despite that fact that the 2005 al-Qaeda bombers included both men and women. Jordan now fears an even greater number of refugees in the event of chaos in Iraq should there be a dangerous setback in the

Iraqi political reconciliation process. A 2007 Jordanian law correspondingly requires Iraqi refugees entering Jordan to carry a G-Series passport.[62] This passport is often much more difficult to obtain than the earlier and more easily forged ones previously used.

Other Regional Countries Hosting Iraqi Refugees.

As noted earlier, sizable numbers of Iraqi refugees have entered Egypt, the Arab Gulf countries, Lebanon, Turkey, and, to a much lesser extent, Iran. While none of these countries are coping with refugee challenges on the scale of Syria and Jordan, a variety of regional states are concerned about the social and economic consequences of accepting additional Iraqis. Egypt, for example, is currently hosting around 150,000 Iraqi refugees, which is manageable for this large Arab country.[63] Nevertheless, the Egyptians are concerned about the danger of a refugee flood similar to that of Jordan and Syria if they allow unlimited access to the country. Cairo has correspondingly limited the entrance of new Iraqi refugees as a result of this concern. Additionally, those Iraqis currently in Egypt have no special status as refugees and no access to Egyptian financial assistance.

The Lebanese leadership is especially concerned about the influx of large numbers of Iraqis. Lebanon has around 50,000 Iraqi refugees, virtually all of whom were there illegally until February 2008, when the government relented on some of its toughest policies and began granting legal status to some refugees.[64] Many others remained in Lebanon illegally. Unlike other Arab countries, Lebanon arrests and imprisons illegal refugees until they agree to return home.[65] The harsh Lebanese reaction to Iraqi refugees may have a great deal to do with the problems that the Lebanese experienced as a result of the presence of between 250,000-420,000 Palestinians in their country.[66]

The huge Iraqi refugee presence in Syria has led to a human smuggling network from Syria into Lebanon for young men seeking work. Many of these men are Shi'ites and place themselves under the protection of the Lebanese Hizballah organization once they arrive in the country.[67] Additionally, Lebanon has gone through a series of recent crises since the February 2005 murder of former Prime Minister Rafik Hariri, including Israel's 2006 war against Hizballah guerrillas operating out of Lebanon. Lebanese political polarization and dysfunctional decisionmaking throughout this period has further undermined the government's ability to deal with Iraqi refugees.

Other regional countries that are hosting smaller numbers of refugees also remain reluctant to open their doors more widely. Turkey currently hosts around 10,000 Iraqi refugees and has been criticized by the UN for returning Iraqis from their border without examining their claims for asylum, as required by international agreements.[68] Kuwait hosts about 15,000 Iraqi refugees and is not interested in allowing this number to increase, partially due to a general distrust of Iraqis and a continuing anger over the 1990 Iraqi invasion of Kuwait and the brutal occupation that followed. In a July 2008 public opinion survey of Kuwaiti citizens, 46 percent of the respondents stated that they opposed the reestablishment of diplomatic relations with Iraq (which had just occurred), and that they would never forgive the Iraqis for their crimes and aggression against Kuwait.[69] The Kuwaitis have indicated that they would provide some financial and logistical support for refugee camps within southern

Iraq if these need to be set up at some point, but they will not accept such camps in Kuwait.[70] Other Gulf countries are willing to accept small numbers of prosperous Iraqis but do not want destitute refugees. Iran remains one of the most interesting possibilities in future scenarios where additional waves of refugees flee Iraq, but it is unclear how Tehran would react to such eventualities.

Future Concerns Regarding Refugees.

As noted, many of the most well-educated and prosperous Iraqi citizens have already fled their country, depriving Iraq of a significant part of its natural leadership and particularly its secular leaders. This exodus is a serious problem for Iraqi reconstruction and political development, but it also has implications for neighboring countries. Under more pessimistic scenarios for Iraqi domestic security, potential future waves of refugees may consist almost entirely of poor and unskilled individuals. Already burdened infrastructures in Syria will need massive international support.

One potentially encouraging trend in recent years has been the return of limited numbers of refugees to Iraq. This transfer has been facilitated with the aid and encouragement of the Iraqi government which has provided bus service from Syria and given families some financial aid to help them relocate back to Iraq.[71] Several apparent reasons are important in helping to cause this change. The most widely suggested one is the improvement in the security conditions in Iraq provided by the 2007 surge in U.S. forces and the U.S. decision to collaborate with former enemies in managing security in the Sunni Arab areas through the Awakening Councils. Some refugees have also considered returning to Iraq as they run out of funds while still failing to find work or otherwise make a living.

Currently, the trickle of returnees is manageable by the Iraqi government and international assistance organizations, although the U.S. military leadership in Baghdad has stated that a massive return of refugees could be destabilizing if it is not properly managed by the government. Some Iraqis who return to their old neighborhoods suggest they would have never done so without the presence of U.S. troops there to keep order.[72] Most external refugees have continued to monitor the situation in Iraq through contact with friends and families by cell phones or, to a lesser extent, through email on the internet. This ongoing contact allows refugees to assess on any changes within the Iraqi political and security situation that might affect the possibility that they can return.

Grave problems will clearly exist for the Iraqi government should large numbers of refugees begin returning home within a limited time span. Such a movement does not appear likely in the near future but could be spurred by a crackdown on refugee movement in either Syria or Jordan. If Syria became unstable itself or experienced ethnic and sectarian warfare on the scale that occurred there in the 1980s, this might also produce refugee movement back to Iraq in significant waves that would be difficult for the country to absorb.

One especially serious problem is that both Shi'ites and Sunnis from mixed neighborhoods will often find these neighborhoods ethnically cleared in ways that do not allow their safe return to their former residences. Even in cases where refugees can safely return to their homes, these same buildings in many cases have been looted, vandalized, or rendered uninhabitable.[73]

AL-QAEDA AND OTHER TERRORIST ACTIVITIES INSIDE IRAQ

The actual and potential expansion of serious terrorist activity across the Middle East as a result of the Iraq conflict is another spillover effect that must be considered when assessing the future of the region. At the time of this writing, international terrorist organizations were suffering serious setbacks within Iraq. In particular, al-Qaeda had deeply alienated itself from its Iraqi allies by 2006, leading many Sunni Iraqi insurgents to break with the terrorist organization and begin cooperating with the United States and, to a lesser extent, the government of Iraq.[74] The decline of al-Qaeda terrorism in Iraq is an extremely positive process, although the potential for Sunni Arab Iraqis to return to cooperation with foreign terrorists should not be dismissed. In a January 2008 interview, General David Petraeus stated that al-Qaeda in Iraq was like a boxer who "has some very serious shots to the head but shakes them off [and] can come back with a very lethal right hand."[75] The widespread defeat or co-optation of Iraqi insurgent forces should help to end Iraq's status as a theater of war in which untrained foreign recruits become professional terrorists and insurgent fighters, while a well-timed and managed drawdown and withdrawal of U.S. troops should reduce some of the rampant anti-Americanism generated throughout the region by the U.S. invasion. Conversely, if al-Qaeda or a successor organization can somehow recover any sort of staying power in Iraq, it will be safe to assume that foreign terrorists will continue to be trained there, and that at least some of these individuals will eventually become involved in other conflicts.

In approaching the danger of a potential rise in regional terrorist activity, it seems clear that terrorism by itself is not Iraq's greatest internal problem. The danger of a breakdown in sectarian relations is a larger long-term problem, and Iraqi-based terrorism is most dangerous to Middle East stability when it is directed at disrupting relations among Iraq's major ethnic and sectarian communities. The future relations among Iraqi's Sunni Arabs, Shi'ite Arabs, and Kurds will correspondingly have a bearing on whether terrorist groups can reestablish themselves in Iraq. Iraq's Sunni Arabs did not turn against al-Qaeda because of their terrorist activities directed against the United States, other regional countries, or Iraq's Shi'ite-dominated government. Rather, many Sunni Arab Iraqis turned against al-Qaeda because of their own communal interests in resisting that organization's attempts to dominate their social, political, and economic lives.[76] In particular, al-Qaeda challenged the role of traditional local leaders, attempted to impose draconian forms of Islamic order on the areas under its control, seized control of Sunni Arab economic resources, and frequently killed anyone who objected to their behavior. A particularly counterproductive strategy was the decision by al-Qaeda members to seek to formalize their involvement in Iraq's Sunni Arab communities through marriages to local women.[77] Additionally, some Sunni fighters aligned with al-Qaeda may have been tempted to change sides simply because they viewed the United States as a more reliable paymaster than al-Qaeda or any other insurgent groups. In a different type of environment, where terrorist groups do not challenge communal interests, some rapprochement may be possible. Therefore, defeating terrorism and sectarian divisions remain directly related to each other.

At the time of this writing, al-Qaeda had been pushed out of many of the areas it formerly controlled by the U.S military, in conjunction with the Iraqi military and the Awakening groups. These groups are composed predominantly of Sunni Arabs and were initially recognized by the United States as "concerned local citizens" in late 2006 and then as the "Sons of Iraq."[78] In early 2008, press reports maintained that there were around 80,000-105,000 Iraqi members of the Awakening groups.[79] The groups are funded at a cost of around $24 million per month which has been paid for by the United States throughout the first years of their existence.[80] The Iraqi government formally agreed to start paying around 50,000 group members starting on October 1, 2008, with the goal of assuming financial responsibility for all of them as soon as possible. Some U.S. officers are uncertain that the government will fully live up to this new responsibility on a continuous basis, and various U.S. military units have been reported to have set aside funds to pay the Awakening forces should the government of Iraq default.[81]

A variety of credible sources have reported that a large number of Iraqi former al-Qaeda fighters have changed sides, and these groups may be dominated by former insurgents.[82] In addition to the insurgents, some members of the Awakening groups are previous members of the Ba'ath party with both military skills and useful intelligence about al-Qaeda.[83] Thus, Shi'ite and Kurdish leaders often distrust them because of their backgrounds as well as their commitment to Sunni interests. By contrast, established Sunni Arab parties such as the Iraqi Islamic Party dislike them because they are emerging as serious rivals for Sunni political leadership. Some Shi'ite leaders have further stated that the Awakening groups will serve as a "fifth column" if they are integrated into the security forces. The Iraqi government consequently has been unwilling to provide them with significant amounts of high quality military weapons, vehicles, and equipment.[84] Baghdad may eventually change this approach due to U.S. pressure, but the underlying hostility between the government and the Awakening groups can be expected to remain and continue to present a problem for counterterrorism efforts in Iraq.

Al-Qaeda's 2006-08 setbacks have dramatically reduced the presence of hostile foreign volunteers within Iraq. This situation is unsurprising since al-Qaeda's welcome was always conditional upon the organization's ability to apply human, financial, and material resources which could be used to advance local Sunni Arab goals. At the beginning of the insurgency, when foreign radicals were especially useful in organizing resistance, local guerrillas accepted foreign radicals playing an important role in the leadership of the anti-government forces. The most notable foreign terrorist leading anti-coalition forces in Iraq at this time was the Jordanian radical Abu Musab al-Zarqawi, who was killed by a U.S. air strike in June 2006. His successor was an Egyptian terrorist fighting under the *nom de guerre* of Abu Ayyab al-Masri.[85] In an apparent effort to manage the strains between Iraqi insurgents and foreign terrorists, al-Masri and other leaders founded an organization called the "Islamic State of Iraq" in 2006. The organization was described on jihadist websites as being led by Abu Omar al-Baghdadi, a name that is identifiably Iraqi. There are no known pictures of Baghdadi and virtually no verifiable information. He may be an actual terrorist leader, but it is also possible that he is a fictional person designed to place an Iraqi face on al-Qaeda's activities in Iraq.[86]

Al-Qaeda's foothold in Iraq may be partially or largely eliminated by the Awakening groups and the U.S. military if current trends continue. It is, however, doubtful that every member of al-Qaeda in Iraq will be killed or captured and that the organization will be fully eradicated, even under the most optimistic of scenarios. Rather, al-Qaeda members may continue operating as small marginalized groups seeking to implement the occasional spectacular terrorist event. They may also attempt to restructure shattered alliances with at least some of Iraq's Sunni Arabs. If they choose the second course, they will have to give up any lingering ideas about dominating Iraq's Sunnis or imposing Taliban-type values on them. Even if al-Qaeda offers these types of concessions, it may still be too late to recreate a working alliance under all but the most exceptional of circumstances. Any future cooperation is likely to be tactical, ad hoc, and characterized by extremely high levels of mutual suspicion, if it occurs at all. The al-Qaeda decision to respond to the rise of the Awakening groups with a wave of assassinations directed against Awakening group leaders and tribal sheikhs also created blood feuds making reconciliation at a later time and under different conditions even more difficult for all involved.

It is also possible that various Iraqi al-Qaeda fighters who are able will simply stop fighting and pursue low profile activities until they feel that opportunities for them to engage in terrorism are more favorable. This approach has sometimes been referred to as a "sleeper cell" scenario.[87] It reflects the difficulty of defeated insurgents pushing forward with large-scale combat activities under conditions where they are harassed by local authorities or under circumstances where a large part of the relevant population is willing to inform against them, as is now the case.[88] Nevertheless, terrorist cells can exist in a number of deeply hostile environments, and the training and expertise necessary to conduct at least some terrorist acts, such as suicide bombings, is often quite minimal. In some cases, al-Qaeda in Iraq has trained individuals as young as 14 for such tasks.[89] It is also possible that the emergence of a new charismatic terrorist leader in Iraq could be particularly relevant to the activation of sleeper cells. Likewise, on a number of occasions in Iraq, al-Qaeda in Iraq has shown that it will intensify the use of car bombs and especially terrorism against "soft targets" such as civilian markets when it is unable to wage warfare effectively against more powerful combatants.[90]

Despite recent victories, the future of the Sunni areas of Iraq has not yet been settled, including their relationship to the Iraqi government and the degree of local Sunni security arrangements acceptable to the central government. The Awakening groups are envisioned by both the U.S. and Iraqi governments to be temporary solutions to the problems of terrorism that will eventually be dissolved. The Maliki government has agreed that only around 20 percent of the Awakening fighters currently under arms will remain as a permanent part of the Iraqi Security Forces once the al-Qaeda threat has been overcome.[91] Most of the groups themselves, however, will probably be reluctant to disarm until they feel that Sunni rights will be scrupulously upheld by the Iraqi government. The potential for problems between the Shi'ite-dominated government and the Sunni tribal areas and their militia defenders will probably remain high after a more comprehensive defeat of al-Qaeda. Any widespread violence between sects in Iraq may create new alliance-building opportunities for terrorists who are willing to help the Sunnis with finances and other resources, provided these groups are actually willing to subordinate themselves to local Iraqi insurgent leaders.

Most Iraqi Sunni fighters view their primary goal as fighting for a future that they view as acceptable for their sect within their own country. This view would inform the outlook of both those individuals fighting for the Awakening groups and Iraqi fighters that remain part of the insurgency. These individuals will correspondingly define victory or defeat through the prism of local and Iraqi circumstances rather than regional or international consequences, and most of these people are unlikely to seek involvement in international terrorist activities outside of Iraq once the current conflict there has ended. Conversely, foreign terrorists who have entered Iraq as part of a "global jihad" have wider agendas and seek a radical transformation of the entire Middle East region. Many of these terrorists may seek involvement in future conflicts once the Iraqi fighting has ended regardless of the outcome of that fighting. The possible rise of a large and growing cadre of committed and professional anti-Western terrorists hardened and professionalized in Iraq and then traveling throughout the world is often viewed as one of the greatest dangers resulting from the continuation of this conflict and the ongoing influx of foreign fighters into the theater of war. Nevertheless, this problem may be manageable by the United States and its allies for reasons noted below.

The capacity of the Iraq conflict to attract volunteers appears to have varied considerably over the course of this ongoing conflict.[92] According to the declassified "key judgments" of a 2006 *National Intelligence Estimate*

(NIE), "The Iraq conflict has become the 'cause celebre' for jihadists, breeding a deep resentment of U.S. involvement in the Muslim world and cultivating supporters for the global jihadist movement."[93] Two years after this NIE, CIA Director General Michael V. Hayden testified before Congress that al-Qaeda was failing because "[d]espite this 'cause celebre' phenomenon, fundamentally no one really liked al-Qaeda's vision of the future."[94] General Hayden maintained that al-Qaeda's form of jihadism was becoming increasingly unpopular and hence joining the conflict in Iraq was a less attractive option. This assertion about al-Qaeda's unpopularity is important, but there are a number of past problems to be overcome before the Iraq issue will lose its saliency among the huge numbers of Arabs and Muslims who view the United States as too intrusive and interventionist.[95] The deep reluctance that the Maliki government displayed in 2008 toward allowing long-term U.S. bases in Iraq is a more benign, but nevertheless unmistakable, indication of Arab distrust of U.S. intentions, and the desire of elected Iraqi politicians to avoid getting on the wrong side of this issue and thereby losing domestic support. As a whole, these factors suggest that the terrorist cause has lost a great deal of its luster for the time being, but underlying distrust of the United States is still strong and exploitable in the Arab world.

There is also the question of how many foreign terrorists have joined the Iraq fighting, survived the years of conflict, and might undertake future operations in Iraq and the wider Middle East. As of July 2008, about 240 foreigners out of 23,000 people were in prison in Iraq for insurgent-related activities, suggesting a 100-to-one ratio based on this interesting, but perhaps not fully representative, sample (since many of the foreign fighters have been reluctant to allow themselves to be taken alive).[96] At various times, foreign militants have been estimated to comprise 4 to 10 percent of the insurgent strength in Iraq with the total Iraqi and foreign insurgent strength reaching a height of 20,000-30,000 fighters in 2005-06. As late as March 2008, U.S. military spokesmen in Iraq stated that non-Iraqi militants constituted around 10 percent of al-Qaeda fighters in Iraq (although not all insurgents are loyal to al-Qaeda).[97] As of mid-2008, al-Qaeda's strength in Iraq was estimated to be between 1,800 to 2,800 combatants, suggesting a total of 180-280 remaining foreign fighters in Iraq. This number can be expected to diminish as U.S. and Iraqi military progress continues.

Many of the foreign terrorists are also believed to have had the highest casualty rates among anti-coalition forces throughout the years of fighting. Up to 90 percent of the suicide bombers in Iraq throughout the conflict are believed to have been foreign radicals. Foreign volunteers with little military background also have higher casualties in many other tactical situations since they would have the steepest learning curve for dealing with unique Iraqi conditions and might often display the greatest enthusiasm for behaving recklessly during combat through activities such as pretending to surrender and then drawing a gun or throwing a grenade.[98] Interestingly, enemy documents captured at Sinjar, near the Syrian border, in September 2007 indicate that most terrorists entering Iraq in recent years were not veterans of previous conflicts such as those in Chechnya, Afghanistan, Kashmir, or elsewhere.[99] Rather, they were usually young men with relatively little life experience and few, if any, military skills. The average age was 24-25, with a few outliers including one 54 year old. This trend underscores the concern expressed in earlier unclassified CIA documents that the most serious terrorism-related danger associated with the conflict is the prospect that Iraq was becoming a center for terrorist professionalization, a place where young unskilled amateurs would be tested with less intelligent and flexible combatants more likely to be killed. Nevertheless, the number of individuals actually surviving this process and moving on to new terrorist activities may be extremely limited.

Currently, it is uncertain how many foreign radicals have been killed in direct fighting with the Awakening Councils, but the numbers could be quite high as al-Qaeda seeks to defend its remaining footholds in Iraq. In such combat, it is doubtful that Iraqi Sunnis in a blood feud against al-Qaeda would show much mercy in the field. Furthermore, the number of foreign fighters entering Iraq is believed to have declined significantly (perhaps to as few as 20 per month), although some of the surviving volunteers who infiltrated earlier are still present in the country.[100] Others have chosen to leave Iraq if they are able to do so. The cause itself may have also lost a great deal of its international appeal following the revolt of Iraqi Sunnis against the al-Qaeda presence in their country. It is much more difficult to mobilize recruits to enter a war where they have a greater chance of fighting fellow Sunni Muslims than American soldiers. Additionally, Iraq's Sunni Arab community is clearly fighting for what it perceives to be its own interests and not on behalf of the Shi'ite-dominated government in Baghdad, further undermining the appeal of joining the al-Qaeda cause in Iraq. One especially interesting indicator of recent al-Qaeda problems is that more jihadist recruiters seem to be facilitating the movement of volunteers to Afghanistan rather than Iraq, because of the changing situations in both countries.[101]

In addition to a dwindling pool of potential volunteers for combat in Iraq, the logistical problems of getting there have increased as a result of added security measures by key countries bordering Iraq, particularly Syria. Syrian border control measures have increased in effectiveness since 2005-06 in ways that have reduced, although not eliminated, the flow of foreign fighters from their territory.[102] One measure cited by General Petraeus in congressional testimony as particularly effective in reducing the flow of foreign fighters has been the Syrian policy of refusing to allow young Arab men to enter the country on one-way airplane tickets unless they are able to prove that their trip is for a purpose other than entering Iraq.[103] This is an unusual step for Syria which traditionally has had a policy of admitting any national from an Arab state without a visa as a gesture of Arab solidarity (despite the 2007 visa requirements previously noted).

Another interesting implication of the improved border security is that al-Qaeda's finances have been deeply crippled since foreign fighters often carried large amounts of money from al-Qaeda supporters when they infiltrated into Iraq. In response, al-Qaeda has increasingly turned to criminal actions such as kidnappings, counterfeiting, hijacking fuel trucks, and extortion to finance its operations within Iraq.[104] Such operations are a distraction from al-Qaeda's main priorities and often require careful planning and the use of resources that al-Qaeda would prefer to apply to the war against the United States and the Iraqi government. These operations can also cause al-Qaeda to make new enemies, although kidnappings and extortion are applied to known enemies whenever possible.

In considering future terrorist operations, any territory under the control of terrorists will be valuable to their organizational efforts, but it may not be essential. The internet has become so key to jihadist struggle that it is possible that it would assume an even more important role in the absence of territorial bases under al-Qaeda control. Additionally, if al-Qaeda can retain safe haven in Pakistan, Afghanistan, or elsewhere, it may not need sanctuary in Iraq to plan and execute operations in the Middle East. For that reason, disrupting financial networks and radical internet activity must continue to be a vital part of the struggle against al-Qaeda which will not end with the U.S. withdrawal from Iraq.

THE POST-IRAQ FUTURE OF THE FOREIGN FIGHTERS

The foreign fighters that have participated in the fighting in Iraq and survived are clearly dangerous people, even if their numbers have not reached the high level that seemed possible prior to the rise of the Awakening groups. Correspondingly, important questions remain about the danger posed by even a limited number of foreign fighters who might emerge from Iraq and seek to create problems elsewhere. In assessing the danger of new waves of terrorists emerging from Iraq, the example of the 1978-89 Afghanistan War is often in the background of any discussion of how fighters hardened in warfare can enter into an ongoing commitment to terrorism against the United States and its allies. Osama bin Laden and many of his followers were deeply involved in the anti-Soviet jihad in Afghanistan, and their experience is sometimes uncritically taken as a template for assessing the future activities of foreign terrorists who are learning military skills in Iraq at the present time. Fighters who gained training and experience in Afghanistan then moved on to other areas of the world to apply the skills that they had gained in the struggle with Soviet forces and pro-Soviet Afghan troops.

Despite some superficial similarities, using the Soviet-Afghan War to predict future terrorism trends emerging from Iraq is an exceptionally unreliable and sloppy form of prediction and analogies between these conflicts must be applied with considerable caution. Serious differences exist between the two situations, and these differences may be further enhanced as the course of the Iraq War evolves. Among the most important differences is that returning fighters from Afghanistan were often viewed with suspicion by their home governments, but they were also generally acknowledged as having participated in a morally acceptable or even virtuous war against Soviet attempts to remold Afghanistan into a communist puppet state. Returnees were watched by local security forces more often than they were imprisoned unless they were caught in subsequent illegal acts within their home country.[105] Some former combatants who did not become involved in criminal or anti-government activities were not persecuted in any way (beyond surveillance and warnings to keep their behavior within acceptable bounds).[106] While the U.S.-led war in Iraq is deeply unpopular in the Arab World, most non-Iraqis who associated themselves with al-Qaeda cannot be expected to receive similar restrained treatment by their home governments. By accepting al-Qaeda's ideology, they have made themselves the enemies of virtually all Arab governments. Most, if not all, of the current Arab regimes have been designated by al-

Qaeda as the "near enemy" (as opposed to the United States—the "far enemy"), and al-Qaeda veterans and associates will probably receive little mercy if caught on the soil of their home countries.[107]

In the case of Afghan war veterans, mercy was sometimes shown to imprisoned terrorists because various Arab governments did not truly know whom they were dealing with and because various Muslim leaders interceded with the government on their behalf. Hence, King Abdullah of Jordan allowed a number of inmates convicted on terrorism-related crimes to go free in a royal amnesty of March 1999 that included Abu Musab al-Zarqawi. The amnesty was announced as a show of royal mercy upon Abdullah becoming king after the death of his father, King Hussein. It is now certain that King Abdullah has learned from this mistake, and other Arab leaders can also be expected to show a dramatically more jaundiced view of mercy for terrorists. Saudi Arabian leaders were also accused of being insufficiently attentive to al-Qaeda activities in their homeland until the organization al-Qaeda in the Arabian Peninsula unleashed a wave of terrorism in Saudi Arabia that was deeply embarrassing and perhaps even threatening to the Saudi regime. In such environments, internal security forces are unlikely to relax their vigilance, and religious leaders would have to consider carefully the implications of calls for mercy (which will almost certainly not be granted). Additionally, the U.S. Government can be expected to be much more involved in efforts to keep track of former fighters from Iraq than they were with militants leaving Afghanistan following the conclusion of the anti-Soviet jihad. At that time, the dominant conflict paradigm was the Cold War and not the danger of terrorism, and the Afghan resistance was sometimes romanticized in the West due to its anti-Soviet efforts.[108]

The worst example of Iraqi-based terrorists striking at a neighboring country was the November 2005 suicide bombing attacks on three Western Hotels in Amman by the Zarqawi organization, in an operation that killed 60 people and wounded 115. This three-pronged strike was horrifying, but it also underscored the difficulties for al-Qaeda in translating terrorist actions into political gains. While the attack was supposed to be directed against U.S. and Israeli interests, the majority of the victims were Arabs, including a number of people attending a wedding reception for a Jordanian couple of Palestinian origins.[109] The Jordanian example also illustrates al-Qaeda's problem in directing terrorism against civilian targets in neighboring countries in ways that are intended to threaten the survival of their governments or place distance between the governments and the population. The hotel bombings did nothing to advance al-Qaeda's goals, and instead provoked an anti-al-Qaeda backlash. The deaths of innocent civilians in the hotel bombings in particular led to a freefall in al-Qaeda's approval ratings among all Jordanians including those of Palestinian origins. Massive demonstrations against al-Qaeda under such banners as "Burn in Hell" underscored the significant opinion shift identified in political polling.[110] Moreover, these opinion shifts against al-Qaeda have endured for years. By attacking civilian targets, al-Qaeda burned its bridges to most public sympathy in Jordan, and it did so with lasting effect. Even radical Jordanians who might have held some sympathy for al-Qaeda's struggle with the U.S. military increasingly came to view the organization as nihilists and criminals.[111]

In explaining the larger context of the terrorism problem in his country, Jordanian King Abdullah stated earlier in 2004 that terrorist networks were being broken up at the rate of one every 2 weeks in his country.[112] Clearly problems emanating from Iraq were a threat to Jordanian security and well-being in this time frame, although it is unclear that terrorists actually need a safe haven in Iraq to plan operations against neighboring governments. The June 2006 death of Zarqawi in a bombing raid, planned with the help of Jordanian intelligence, may have slowed the terrorist vendetta against Amman.[113] Jordan appears to have been able to confine the problem of high casualty terrorist attacks to only one serious and simultaneous set of attacks because of the professionalism that its intelligence and security forces showed once they fully understood the nature and magnitude of the danger.[114]

Despite the problems for al-Qaeda that can be seen with the Jordanian case, militants with experience fighting in Iraq have turned up in other Middle Eastern conflicts, and they are still capable of causing serious problems. In contrast to the situation in Jordan, these forces can present special difficulties in divided countries with weak governments and uncertain internal security forces. One 2007 battleground where foreign terrorists were a serious problem is the Nahr al-Bared refugee camp outside of Tripoli, Lebanon, where al-Qaeda-inspired Palestinian guerrillas and their supporters fought a 4-month series of battles with the Lebanese Army.[115] Over 400 people were killed in this fighting, and the Lebanese Army was severely tested by the fervent resistance of the guerrillas.[116] More than 160 soldiers were killed, and a large number were wounded. [117] According to Palestinian journalist Rami Khouri, Fatah Islam was led by former Palestinian guerrillas but also had numerous international jihadists from Arab and Asian countries.[118] Major General Achraf Rifi, the general director of Lebanon's

Internal Security Forces, stated that as many as 50 Iraq war veterans fought in the battles at Nahr al-Bared.[119] If this statement is correct, it is a particularly dramatic example of Iraq's foreign volunteers plying their skills elsewhere in a way that threatened a friendly government.

Also, the U.S. Embassy in Yemen was attacked with rocket propelled grenades, vehicle bombs, and automatic weapons fire on September 17, 2008. The well-organized and well-coordinated nature of the attack caused a U.S. Government spokesman to state that it "bears all the hallmarks of an al-Qaeda attack."[120] Currently, it is not known if any of the attackers had previous experience in Iraq, although more details should become known as the police investigation continues.

THE DANGER OF SPILLOVER SECTARIANISM STRIFE

Rising Sunni-Shi'ite sectarian tension appears to be an increasingly alarming trend in many Middle East societies and has been aggravated by a number of factors including (but not confined to) the Iraq War and the rise of a Shi'ite-led government in Baghdad. Sectarian tensions have existed in a variety of Middle Eastern states throughout recent decades, and causality for recent upsurges cannot be attributed to a single foreign or domestic factor. Some Arab states, such as Kuwait, have made serious efforts to integrate the Shi'ites into national life. Other nations, including Saudi Arabia, have been slower and more uncertain about accepting the Shi'ites into national life in ways that respect their rituals and traditions. Nevertheless, the politicization of sectarian differences within Iraq that followed the destruction of the dictatorship is one of the most virulent dangers threatening the wider region. Moreover, the increased political power and status of the Iranian regime and its allies, which occurred as an unintended side effect of the Iraqi invasion and rising price of oil, has further enhanced this danger.

Sectarianism has a long and unpleasant history in Iraq that has been expressed in a variety of different ways.[121] Under Saddam Hussein any assertion of sectarian grievances was treated as sedition designed to weaken the Iraqi nation and encourage disorder and division in cooperation with various hostile powers — particularly the United States and Israel.[122] In the early stages of the coalition military occupation of Iraq, the danger of politicizing sectarian differences was not always well-understood and was often minimized by outsiders observing Iraqi society. One of the most frequently cited reasons for this complacency about sectarian differences involved the supposedly high numbers of "mixed" sectarian marriages. According to more recent sources, the number of these marriages was greatly exaggerated.[123] Moreover, the presence of mixed marriages should not be taken as a serious barrier to escalating civil strife. In other civil conflict situations, such couples have been forced to take sides at some point and are not given the option of remaining neutral. In some extreme cases, relatives and even spouses turn against each other in situations of ethnic or sectarian conflict.[124]

The rise of political sectarianism in Iraq since 2003 has now become a well-known story. Long simmering grievances came to the surface of the Iraqi political system in ways that threatened the stability of the state once the dictatorship was removed. Moreover, and perhaps more significantly, the post-invasion security environment led many Iraqis to seek some form of local protection which invariably involved armed groups of their own sect, even under circumstances where these groups victimized as well as protected them.[125] Elections in Iraq tended to further confirm political polarization, with various observers noting that voting results looked more like a census of Iraq's ethnic and sectarian breakdown than an election based on a larger range of issues.[126] Political parties that attempted to appeal to voters across ethnic and sectarian divides were almost entirely marginalized as occurred in the case of former Iraqi Prime Minister Ayad Allawi's Iraq National List coalition of political parties, which achieved a disappointing 15 percent of the total vote.[127] Political leaders competing to lead a party based on the interests of only one sectarian group often had little incentive to make concessions to other groups and then attempt to explain these concessions to their domestic constituency. Using these problems as a backdrop, al-Qaeda in Iraq had a deliberate policy of attempting to foment sectarian strife in order to render the country ungovernable and, according to Abu Musab al-Zarqawi, "awaken the inattentive Sunnis" to the danger of Iraqi Shi'ites dominating Iraq.[128]

By 2006, Iraq appeared to be inching towards full-scale sectarian war. A variety of factors managed to prevent this from occurring. As noted earlier, the U.S. military surge strategy is usually given the largest amount of credit for rolling back the danger of a full scale civil war, and it clearly had a serious positive impact at least for the short term. Another perhaps more important factor was the willingness of former insurgents in the Awakening groups to turn against al-Qaeda in exchange for U.S. funding and support, and to reestablish the dominance of tribal leaders in their own provinces at the expense of al-Qaeda and the Iraqi central government. A further positive factor was the decision by Shi'ite leader Muqtada al-Sadr to stand down his militia for an extended time following a reckless and embarrassing shootout with Iraqi police in August 2007 in the Holy City of Karbala. The March 2008 partial defeat of Sadr's militia by Iraqi government forces also damaged Sadr's overall political strength, although it is not clear how extensive or lasting these setbacks will be for the Sadr movement.[129] In addition, by 2008 many mixed neighborhoods in Baghdad and other cities had become increasingly segregated, with members of one or the other sect abandoning their homes rather than being threatened or killed by hostile militias. This process of division, while tragic for many families who have lost their homes, nevertheless reduced the killing by separating the combatants. In describing such sectarian polarization, Sunni black humor maintains that the only members of their sect to enter Shi'ite areas, such as the Sadr City area of Baghdad, do so in the trunks of cars.[130]

In Sunni-dominated Arab countries, fear of Shi'ite militancy spreading to Iraq's neighbors is intensifying because of the emotional impact of violence between Iraqi sects. More importantly, the Iraqi government which came to power after the 2005 elections is the first Shi'ite-dominated government established in the Arab World for over 800 years.[131] This development is unwelcome for a variety of regimes where Shi'ites have political and economic grievances and especially among the Gulf monarchies. The February 2006 al-Qaeda bombing of the Askari Shi'ite Mosque and shrine in Samarra dramatically increased the level of violence in Iraq, with retaliatory strikes on approximately 200 Sunni mosques throughout Iraq within a week of the attack.[132] While sectarian violence in Iraq has declined from the level of 2006, it remains exceptionally serious and could still serve as the basis for escalating civil conflict at a later time. Moreover, while the large-scale segregation of Sunnis and Shi'ites into different areas has reduced the present level of violence, it has also created new grievances among large numbers of Iraqi citizens who have lost their homes. It is unclear how these grievances may manifest themselves in the future.

Middle Eastern Sunni-Shi'ite differences in the recent past have often been at least partially linked to the state of relations between Iran and the Arab World. The most important example of this trend was the 1979 Iranian Revolution which was viewed by some Arab Shi'ites as an empowering event. According to Yitzhak Nakash, a leading scholar of Shi'ite politics, Saudi Arabian Shi'ites regard the era following the Iranian revolution as the most difficult in their recent history because of Saudi Arabian government suspicion and repression, as well as the escalating hostile rhetoric of Saudi Arabia's Sunni clerics.[133] Moreover, the escalation of government repression helped to render the Saudi Shi'ites more receptive to Iranian propaganda. Reconciliation occurred between the government and Shi'ite community leaders in 1993, but bitterness and continuing anti-Shi'ite discrimination remain, albeit at lower levels.[134] This problem also occurred in some Gulf Arab countries during the Iran-Iraq War when many Shi'ites were viewed as potentially sympathetic to Iran's efforts to encourage armed opposition to anti-Iranian Sunni monarchies.[135] Since Saddam Hussein's ouster in 2003, Iran once again sees itself on the rise as it has emerged as the dominant regional power in the Gulf. This potential new threat is deeply unsettling to those Arab states that have traditionally maintained concerns about Iranian radicalism.[136] Some Arab states are also concerned that Iran is exploiting its enhanced role in ways that threaten their position in the region and future internal security. Such domestic concerns may once again lead various Arab governments to initiate or intensify discrimination against their Shi'ite citizens especially in administrative and security-related employment due to fear that they are not trustworthy and more likely than other citizens to serve as Iranian agents. Such discrimination would inevitably lead to Shi'ite alienation, which could perhaps result in more government repression reigniting the familiar vicious circle.

The concept of a monolithic Shi'ite bloc led by Iran seems farfetched because of the factors preventing it including Shi'ite factionalism, domestic politics, nationalistic concerns, international politics, and economics. The accusation that such a bloc would consist of a variety of Arab states and political movements led by Iran, a non-Arab power, is also unusual, and such an alliance is difficult to see as enduring and durable. Nevertheless, such concerns are very real, and even an ephemeral Iranian-led Shi'ite alliance concerns many moderate Middle Eastern leaders. In its most extreme manifestations, conservative Arab leaders who are worried about a Shi'ite bloc tend to fear that Iran will dominate Iraq, Syria, and key nonstate actors including the Shi'ite Lebanese group, Hizballah, and the even the Sunni Palestinian group, Hamas. Hamas has strong ties to Iran for political and economic rather than sectarian reasons.[137] Syria and Iran are currently allies and have a long history of cooperation.

Many of Iraq's neighbors have made a number of strong statements about the need for them to cooperate among themselves (and when possible with Iraq) to stem the danger of cross border terrorism and agitation of sectarian unrest emanating from Iraq. Central to this approach is a professed desire for coordination, cooperation, and intelligence exchanges with other countries that feel threatened by developments in Iraq.[138] Some of this coordination is going forward, and there are even some press reports that Israel has been involved in limited intelligence-sharing with Arab states opposing Iranian influence in the region.[139] Nevertheless, intelligence-sharing with other countries is often a painful process that is difficult to move forward. While virtually all states are happy to receive information of value, most states are equally loath to pass on their most carefully protected secrets to other nations. Such cooperation is also limited by the differing levels of credibility among the intelligence services of various states. Many intelligence organizations can be expected to be reluctant to share their own sensitive information with organizations that they view as having little to offer in return. It is possible that fear of Iran will help to overcome some of this reluctance, but this is by no means certain.

Kuwait, which is led by a Sunni monarchy, has accurately been described as being the most tolerant of the Gulf societies towards Shi'ites and the most willing to allow its Shi'ite citizens to integrate into society. Yet, even in this more liberal Gulf society, sectarian concerns have sometimes moved to the forefront of domestic politics. In February 2008, for example, the government reacted with apprehension and anger to a well-attended rally to mourn the death of former Lebanese Hizballah commander Imad Mughniyah, who had just been assassinated in a car bombing in Syria widely believed to be conducted by the Israelis.[140] By this time, Mughniyah was probably not an active Hizballah leader, but he is widely believed to have had a great deal of Israeli blood on his hands, and his death may have been an exercise in Israeli revenge and accountability rather than part of a struggle against important and dangerous terrorists.[141] Nevertheless, many Sunni Kuwaitis were not sorry to see him killed since he had also been implicated in the murder of two Kuwaiti citizens during a 1988 airplane hijacking in which the bodies were dumped on the tarmac of Larnaca Airport in Cyprus.[142]

Despite the ugly aspects of Hizballah's history, many Kuwaiti Shi'ites view it as an especially heroic organization in its struggle against Israel and treat Hizballah deeds as a source of Shi'ite pride. During the rally noted above, one Shi'ite member of the Kuwaiti National Assembly referred to Mughniyah as a "martyr hero," leading to accusations that he and another Shi'ite Member of Parliament (MP) were actually members of "Hizballah Kuwait," an organization that is not known to have been active since the latter years of the 1980-88 Iraq-Iraq War. Some Sunni MPs suggested that the organizers of the rally should have been stripped of their parliamentary status so that they could be placed on trial. In response, Speaker of the Parliament Jassem al-Khorafi criticized what he called the "exaggerated reaction to the mourning rally," and played a valuable role in calming the situation.[143] He also stated that attacks on the national loyalty of the Shi'ites is a problem which held the danger of "demolishing the future of the country."[144] Yet, some bitterness clearly remained. In a particularly bitter reflection of anger over Sunni distrust, one Shi'ite commentator stated, "If you're a [Shi'ite] in Kuwait, you have to swear five times a day after each prayer that you hate Iran and love Israel."[145]

Iraq's only neighboring country with a Shi'ite Arab majority population is Bahrain. Bahrain is governed by a Sunni Arab monarchy, although around 60-65 percent of its population are Shi'ite Arabs (down from around 70 percent due to extensive naturalizations of Sunnis born outside of Bahrain). Many Shi'ites in Bahrain feel that they are the victims of serious discrimination in government hiring and economic programs directed at their community, as well as a general lack of political power. Domestic problems rather than Iraq-related issues currently seem to be the most serious source of division between the two communities. Nevertheless, Bahrain's Sunni leadership is often viewed as insensitive to the problems of the Shi'ite community, and an effort to more evenly distribute government jobs and economic assistance could help immensely in causing Shi'ites to buy into the political system in ways that help to minimize any future problems that might emerge in parallel to intercommunal relations in Iraq following an eventual U.S. withdrawal from that country. Interestingly, the United Arab Emirates (UAE), with its sizable 17 percent Shi'ite minority (including many noncitizens), shows no signs of serious Sunni-Shi'ite tension, despite the government's good relations with the United States.[146]

SECESSIONIST THREATS

Iraq currently faces a potential secessionist sentiment from its Kurdish citizens which will either be effectively managed or spin out of control, depending upon future developments in Iraqi domestic politics and the effectiveness of national reconciliation efforts. Worldwide, Kurds are the largest national group without their own country, and many Kurds have developed a fierce nationalism and separatist identity partially based on this unfulfilled dream. In Iraq, they constitute around 5 million people, or 15-20 percent of the population. Since 2003, Iraqi Kurds have been able to pursue a remarkably effective policy of maximizing their influence in the Baghdad central government while still making significant strides towards bypassing the authority of the national government in the Kurdish areas. Iraqi Kurds are making a fairly undisguised effort to achieve a high level of autonomy which borders on *de facto* independence. Moreover, the weakness of the central government has allowed the Kurds to make considerable progress towards obtaining this goal. Shortly after Saddam's fall, a special Kurdish Regional Government (KRG) was established for the three Iraqi provinces that currently comprise Kurdistan. This government negotiates foreign business agreements, issues visas, and maintains its own army, which has only the most tentative ties to the military command in Baghdad. The flying of the Iraqi national flag was not permitted in the two main Kurdish-dominated cities of Irbil and Sulaymaniah from 2003 until early 2008, but it was flown later after three stars representing the Ba'ath party were removed from the flag.[147]

Kurdish longing for independence will probably remain fundamental to the Iraqi Kurdish outlook for the foreseeable future. Kurdish actions on this issue will probably be opportunistic based upon how much autonomy they can seize without producing angry and effective reactions from the Baghdad government. A strong central government of any kind in Baghdad has always concerned the Kurds, and the majority of Iraqi Kurds would be particularly interested in maintaining their political distance from an Islamist government that would seek to impose a rigid system of religious conformity throughout the country.[148] The activities of Muqtada al-Sadr's movement have been of special concern to the Kurds because of Sadr's militant ideas and because he has a following among many Shi'ite Arabs who were relocated to northern Iraq under Saddam's "Arabization" program for northern Iraq. Should the Sadrists gain control of the Baghdad government, the Kurds would be further energized to resist central government authority.

An additional complication for Arab-Kurdish relations is that at least 40 percent of Iraq's oil infrastructure is in the northern part of the country. To exploit these resources, the Kurdish bloc in parliament has strongly favored a draft national oil law which invites regional governments to sign their own oil contacts and to welcome economic joint ventures with Baghdad's approval.[149] This prospective law was never enacted into legislation, and at the time of this writing Iraq had no laws addressing the major questions surrounding the conduct of its energy sector, although this deadlock does not mean that there is no activity on oil exploitation. Rather, the KRG has attempted to fill this gap by passing its own legislation on oil and natural gas, which unsurprisingly provides a maximalist interpretation of local rights. The Kurds then moved forward to negotiate an estimated 25 contracts with foreign energy firms. The oil deals appear designed to help Iraqi Kurds build their own economic base in the north while oil legislation remains bogged down in the national parliament. This approach sets an alarming precedent for other provincial governments which may be interested in signing contracts with foreign governments in a variety of fields, thereby further undermining the central government. The Iraqi government has signaled its hostility to the independent Kurdish agreements and has hinted that it may blacklist and exclude oil companies that conclude agreements with the KRG unless they give up their unauthorized agreements with them.[150]

Faced with determined government opposition to independent oil deals, Kurdish leaders have shown some hints of flexibility. Most notably, the central government and the KRG set up a joint panel in June 2008 to resolve differences on oil-related issues. This panel includes Prime Minister Maliki and KRG Premier Nechirvan Barzani.[151] The panel's creation is a potentially useful step, especially since its membership includes top level officials who do not need to seek the approval of higher authorities for their actions. Nevertheless, the simplest way to imply progress on an issue where none exists is to create a bureaucratic entity such as a joint panel. It is by no means clear that such an organization will be able to avoid unproductive bickering and instead resolve highly divisive issues.

A central issue in Iraq's ethnic tension centers on the city of Kirkuk and, to a lesser extent, some of the areas around the city of Mosul.[152] Virtually all Iraqi Kurds consider Kirkuk to be their "Jerusalem" and state that its inclusion into the Kurdistan region is an issue upon which they will not compromise.[153] The city, however, is not currently part of the Kurdish region, and its future remains unresolved. The Iraqi government has failed to hold the referendum on the future status of Kirkuk that the Iraqi Constitution required to take place before December 31, 2007. This vote was postponed until June 2008, but it did not take place then either. Arab and Turkmen (also called Turcomen) groups in the area now argue that the deadline has been missed for a referendum, and it should not be held.[154] Many Arabs moved to Kirkuk as a result of the Ba'ath party's large-scale "Arabization" campaign which began in

1963 and then expanded during the 1970s. These Arab residents currently fear that they will be compelled to leave Kirkuk if it is incorporated into the Kurdish region as a result of the referendum.[155] These mostly Shi'ite residents are known as "10,000" by the Kurds due to Saddam's offer of 10,000 dinars and housing in exchange for their commitment to migrate to the north, displacing Kurds and Turkmens. Many came from the slum area of what is now Sadr City, often with the hope of working in Iraq's oil industry. Shi'ites from the slums often viewed such opportunities as one of their only chances for a decent life.

As the Kurds appear increasingly interested in political control of the north, Iraq's other communities have become deeply and increasingly concerned. Sunni and Shi'ite Arab political parties which have seldom been able to cooperate on other important issues are united in their efforts to contain Kurdish efforts to distance themselves from the Iraqi central government. This tension has also fed inter-ethnic distrust, and it is therefore not surprising that Kirkuk has been home to a powerful and active Sunni Arab terrorist underground which may have been strengthened in reaction to increased Kurdish power.[156] In other areas of the north, including the city of Mosul, Sunni Arabs who feel their rights threatened have been particularly receptive to the possibility of joining al-Qaeda or other insurgent organizations before these organizations became unwelcome in Iraq's Sunni areas. The potential for these disaffected individuals to view some acts of terrorism in a positive way can be expected to remain so long as Kurdish-Arab tensions are unresolved. Moreover, a disproportionate number of Sunni Arab army officers have come from Mosul since the early history of the country.[157] This military tradition has led to a great deal of military expertise among those Mosul citizens who once served in the Iraqi army disbanded by the United States in 2003.

Neighboring countries also worry that Iraqi Kurds are threatening their own national unity in addition to the unity of Iraq. Turkey is clearly deeply concerned about the prospect of an independent Kurdish state which would gain allies and diplomatic clout through the export of significant amounts of oil. The Ankara government, and especially the Turkish military leadership, considers preventing the emergence of a Kurdish state fundamental to its national interests. According to journalist Quil Lawrence, Turkish officials have told Washington that they fear that a strong, oil rich, Kurdish state in northern Iraq could "start stealing swaths of southeastern Turkey" probably by supporting insurgent groups such as the Kurdish Workers' Party (PKK).[158] While this may seem unlikely to Western observers, the emotional intensity of the Turks on the issue is difficult to miss, especially since the PKK fought a long and bloody sectarian war with the Turkish army from 1984 until 1999.[159] The Turkish leadership has also made a number of statements suggesting that they consider the Iraqi KRG complicit in terrorism. Turkey's ambassador to Washington claims Iraqi Kurds support the PKK "not only with safe havens, but with logistics, weapons, ammunition, and explosives."[160]

Under these conditions, Turkish military posturing is continuous, and Ankara's resort to force often occurs quickly. There have been approximately 25 serious Turkish military cross-border operations into northern Iraq since 1984.[161] Some of these efforts have been serious military offensives such as a March 1995 strike involving 35,000 troops and penetrating 35 miles into Iraq on a 150-mile front. Shortly before the 2003 fighting began, Turkey threatened to intervene throughout northern Iraq if Kurdish troops were used to capture either Kirkuk or Mosul, but Ankara did not do so when Kurdish forces did participate in the capture of Kirkuk.[162] Limited incursions continued throughout the post-Saddam era, although they offered only short-lived gains as the PKK regrouped and reorganized. In a more recent large-scale operation beginning on December 16, 2007, Turkish air raids against the PKK in Iraq began with some regularity, and ground operations were initiated on February 21, 2008. This incursion, designated as Operation Sun, lasted 8 days. While initial media reports suggested that approximately 10,000 Turkish troops were involved, this estimate appears to have been vastly inflated with 2,000 ground troops being a more accurate number.[163] Turkish military action has usually been confined to border regions, although Ankara has at times threatened more sweeping military intervention, to include Kirkuk, to protect the Turkmen minority there.[164] Such intervention cannot reasonably be expected to occur with U.S. troops in Iraq, but the threats could become much less farfetched following a U.S. withdrawal should order break down in the north or large-scale organized violence be directed at the Turkmens.

As noted, the Turkish leadership maintains that their problems with the PKK have increased as a result of Iraqi Kurdish support to the PKK. Some Turkish academics have, however, counseled flexibility in dealing with the Iraqi Kurds, and favored the idea of seeking what amounts to a Turkish protectorate over the north if full-scale civil war breaks out in Iraq. This approach assumes that the Kurds would have little choice other than to accept such an outcome. Such ideas build on previous suggestions by former Turkish

President Turgut Ozal who died in 1993. According to Ozal,

> [A Kurdish state in northern Iraq] would be totally dependent on Turkey because how else would they export or import their goods? The Iraqis would surely be pretty mad at them, so they'd be dependent on Turkey. For Kurds in Turkey, the government would be able to say, "If you'd like to live in a Kurdish state, there's one . . . And if you'd like to live here, these are the rules."[165]

A Kurdish dependence in northern Iraq would also help buffer Turkey from any radical activity and Islamist activity emerging from the Arab areas of Iraq.

In addition to Turkey, the Iranian leadership is also apprehensive about anti-Iranian Kurdish separatist groups which operate in alliance with the PKK and appear to be organizing their military forces without any interference from local Iraqi Kurds. The largest of the anti-Iranian Kurdish movements is the Kurdistan Free Life Party (PJAK), which also has forces in the Qandil Mountains in Iraq. This group was formed in 2004 and has conducted raids into Iran since at least the beginning of 2007.[166] They may also be responsible for shooting down an Iranian helicopter in February 2008 in which General Saeed Qahhari and several other senior leaders of the Iranian Revolutionary Guards Corps were killed.[167] Iran has responded to this threat with artillery strikes and even commando raids into northern Iraq.[168] The Iranians, however, must be much more careful than the Turks when conducting such operations since the United States views the Tehran government to be an enemy regime with an often hostile agenda in Iraq.

CRIMINAL ACTIVITIES OUTSIDE OF IRAQ LINKED TO THE IRAQI WAR

Criminal and quasi-criminal militia groups have helped to fill the power vacuum in Iraq since 2003. Serious problems involving crime and lawlessness have influenced all of the spillover problems noted above in a variety of ways. Criminals can be particularly helpful to terrorists with a number of services including money laundering, forging documents, obtaining illegal weapons, and other such assistance. In some cases, kidnappers have sold kidnapped individuals to terrorists if they have political importance.[169] Some criminal activities are linked to sectarian militias which seek political power. It is not always clear when a militia organization has stopped being a paramilitary group and has fully evolved into a criminal organization without ideology. Some sectarian militias are extremely forceful in enforcing contributions by members of their community in the areas that they control. Additionally, Iraq's long-standing problems with lawlessness, including the problem of kidnappings, have been a major contributing factor to refugee flight.

Iraqi organized criminal networks that operate primarily for profit seem to have developed in a variety of ways. The first type of network consists of criminal organizations that were involved in smuggling and black market activities under the sponsorship and protection of the Saddam Hussein regime while it was in power.[170] Regime-sponsored programs to obtain contraband goods abroad have a long history. During the 1980-88 Iran-Iraq War, the Iraqis maintained an extensive clandestine procurement network to obtain a variety of controlled technologies that were useful for the war effort and Saddam's then-viable chemical, biological, and nuclear weapons programs. Later, smuggling, and especially the smuggling of oil exports, was an important part of the regime's effort to circumvent UN sanctions and generate funds for its continuation in power.[171] Corrupt procurement networks correspondingly became an important part of the Saddamist system with pro-regime operatives operating from foreign centers of commerce including Amman and Beirut.[172]

Some of these pro-Saddam organizations continued with their illegal operations after his ouster. Additionally, Sunni Arab tribes in western Iraq were involved in a variety of lucrative smuggling activities while the Ba'ath regime was in power, and continued with these types of activities afterwards. Al-Qaeda's effort to seize control of these enterprises was an important reason for Sunni tribal estrangement from foreign terrorists. Saddam tolerated this activity because he considered these tribes to be heavily composed of regime allies.[173] Elsewhere in Iraq, some observers suggest that criminal activity constituted the majority of the violence in Shi'ite areas in the immediate aftermath of the 2003 invasion since most Shi'ites were at that time ready to adopt a wait and see attitude toward the coalition presence.[174]

Problems with criminality were also severely aggravated in the lead up to the U.S.-led invasion of Iraq. In October 2002, Saddam released around 75,000 to 100,000 criminals from prison in the probable expectation that they would complicate any effort by the United States to install a new regime in Iraq. The only major group that appears to have been excluded from this amnesty were political prisoners who were deemed to be a danger or an embarrassment to the regime.[175] The prisoners released in October 2002 have been described as a "professional class in armed robbery, carjacking, kidnapping, rape, and, if the price was right, murder."[176] Some of these released convicts returned to crime as individuals or in small groups, while others were to practice their craft with the protection and assistance of organized criminal groups who were provided with a share of the profits. Many benefited from the easy availability of firearms and military weapons including machine guns and rocket propelled grenades (RPGs). The almost complete collapse of all border controls in the aftermath of the invasion also created serious problems.[177] The breakdown of law and order as well as border security allowed Iranian and other foreign-based criminal networks to expand their influence into Iraq. The Iranian criminals, in particular, may have seen Iraq as a valuable market for future drug sales since drug abuse among ordinary citizens was virtually unheard of during Saddam's regime because it was suppressed with unrelenting ferocity.[178]

The ingredients for an explosion in criminal activity were therefore present in 2003 when the police system collapsed in the aftermath of the coalition invasion. The police under the Ba'ath were corrupt and ineffective, but the almost complete disappearance of even these marginal law enforcement forces compounded the threat to social order. Only the traffic police remained intact as a functioning national organization.[179] Other national police dispersed into the population. While the coalition forces sought to correct this problem, there were also massive difficulties in reestablishing police units since they were seen as a sign of expanding Iraqi government authority and were heavily targeted by insurgents. In some cases, police stations were attacked by insurgents, with heavy casualties inflicted on the defenders. In a variety of instances, the insurgents were better armed than the police. In the early post-Saddam years, the insurgents made a special effort to portray these forces as stooges of an occupying power. In response to this highly threatening environment, some police officers tried to hide their identity for fear of retribution against themselves and their families. Other police officers and units were extremely reluctant to leave their stations which they considered to be under siege.

The Iraqi government also became even more deeply mired in corruption following Saddam's ouster. Corrupt practices had previously been contained by the repressive apparatus of Saddam Hussein's unforgiving internal security practices and the atmosphere of fear that they created. Corruption, while an integral part of the Saddamist system, could be safely practiced only with regime sanction and in ways that did not compete with the corrupt activities of Iraq's top leadership, such as Uday Hussein. The removal of the Saddam regime allowed what one former post-Saddam Iraqi minister referred to as an "exponential increase in corruption."[180] It especially allowed an increase in the number of people who could and did become involved in large-scale corrupt practices because they no longer had to worry about offending powerful and merciless government leaders. The problem of instability also contributed to problems with corruption since many Iraqis felt that they might be forced to flee Iraq under certain circumstances, and no one wanted to be without resources if that decision was forced upon them. Under these circumstances, virtually all criminal activity has benefited from the collapse of law enforcement institutions and the massive corruption in the government which makes senior officials susceptible to the blandishments and opportunities presented by organized crime.[181] Moreover, in conditions of impoverishment, questions about how money is obtained can often go unasked.

Muqtada al-Sadr's Mahdi Army has deeply infiltrated the police in a variety of cities, including Baghdad. Some of these police officers are known to be deeply corrupt and have the additional protection of their government status, as well as various militia friendly senior officers or officers who are afraid of the militias. Various splinter groups from the Mahdi Army are often viewed as little more than criminal gangs with few ties to the main organization. Spokesmen for the Mahdi Army claim that criminals who were never part of the Mahdi Army are impersonating members of their organization.[182] Additionally, Sadr has appealed to his followers not to engage in criminal activity, but neither he nor they appear to take these statements very seriously.[183] Nor is it clear that the Mahdi Army could stay away from corruption even if its leadership found this appealing. Sadr's need to pay and field a militia, as well as provide social services to large numbers of Shi'ites in Baghdad and southern Iraq, would make any source of funds important to him. Currently, most of the Mahdi Army's funds come from both voluntary and coerced "donations" from Shi'ites living in areas under its control. Additionally, it has confiscated significant amounts of property from Sunnis whom it has driven out of their former homes.

Criminal groups and professional smugglers have also facilitated the movement of jihadi recruits traveling from foreign countries into Iraq to join the fight against the Iraqi government and coalition forces according to the Sinjar documents cited earlier in this report. These documents suggest that jihadists most often attempted to join the current struggle by entering Syria and were then met by al-Qaeda supporters and facilitators at various locations, including the Damascus Airport. Professional criminals, and not ideological comrades, were then utilized to cross the Syrian border into Iraq. The Syrian government is widely believed to be aware of this activity, but has practiced what the Iraq Study Group has called "malign neglect" which they define as "look[ing] the other way as arms and foreign fighters flow across their border into Iraq . . . "[184] Since that time, Syrian cooperation in controlling the borders and the movement of radicals is reported to have significantly increased in response to the U.S. presence.

Another terrorism related problem is that Iraq is awash with firearms and other weapons which may be smuggled to a variety of Iraq's neighbors. According to the U.S. Government Accountability Office (GAO), 190,000 assault weapons and pistols provided to the Iraq Security Forces in 2004 and 2005 are officially lost or missing.[185] Some of these weapons may have been destroyed in combat, but many others have made their way to the Iraqi black market. The breakdown of these missing weapons includes 110,000 AK-47s and 80,000 pistols. While the pistols would not add much to insurgent firepower, they are often a weapon of choice for assassination and urban terrorism. The provision of large numbers of weapons to members of the Awakenings organizations may have the unexpected side effect of having many of these same weapons be taken by or sold to terrorists.

Iraq is not currently a major smuggling route for illegal narcotics, although there are some potential reasons why criminals might find it attractive for such purposes at a later date. Currently, Afghan opiates are most often smuggled though Pakistan, Iran, and some of the former Soviet republics to reach western and other markets.[186] Corrupt Iraqi crime lords and militia leaders may nevertheless be willing to become involved in this trade if they are able to obtain an acceptable share of the profit. If politically powerful Iraqi leaders develop a strong and profitable relationship with the international drug industry, Iraq's role in the drug trade may become especially difficult to roll back at a later point. Political leaders who help to finance their activities with drug money could be expected to use all of their influence to prevent serious government efforts to control this problem, and could corrupt the national government on this issue in ways similar to trends that are sometimes reported to exist in Afghanistan.[187]

Iraqi criminal networks would probably be most interested in helping to service the lucrative and expanding illegal drug market in the Gulf area. The Gulf States have been identified as having both a growing market for drugs, and as states that lack a legal infrastructure and regional counternarcotics cooperation to address the challenge of well-organized drug traffickers. Many of these states do, however, have tough policies for convicted drug traffickers, including the use of the death penalty. The use of harsh punishment may have some value as a deterrent, but is often viewed by criminal networks as part of the cost of doing business and a certain number of people are expendable.[188] If Iraqi criminals make inroads into this market, they may then seek to expand operations into whatever other markets are available. Additionally, young Iraqi militia members, as well as members of criminal gangs, are sometimes known to abuse drugs. The trend is believed to be strongest in organizations where religious figures have lost their authority to more streetwise individuals.[189]

CONCLUSIONS AND POLICY RECOMMENDATIONS

It is inevitable that civil unrest and other problems in Iraq would have spillover effects for other regional countries. These problems will continue even if the situation in Iraq steadily improves and will become especially problematic if the situation in Iraq deteriorates. Virtually every responsible person dealing with Iraq acknowledges that gains in that country are fragile and reversible and that ultimately the Iraqis and not the Americans will decide the Iraqi future. It is, therefore, vital that the United States prepares for spillover problems beyond Iraq's borders, and that this is done in the knowledge that the road to a unified and stable Iraq remains long and uncertain. Even temporary and reversible disasters in Iraq can have catastrophic results for U.S. interests in the Middle East if efforts to address Iraqi spillover are not adequate. The following policy recommendations are therefore offered with this situation in mind.

1. U.S. civilian and military planners need to remain sensitive to the possibility that the most dangerous spillover threat from Iraq is ethnic and sectarian conflict, and if such spillover occurs in any dramatic way, it may be catastrophic for U.S. interests. Sectarian hatreds can lead to civil unrest and undermine the stability of countries beyond Iraqi borders. Moreover, the United States must accept the possibility of a long-term struggle between Iraq's Sunnis and Shi'ites which intensifies dramatically once U.S. forces leave Iraq, regardless of how many years they remain and attempt to "fix" the political system. The potential for such problems spreading is directly related to the discontent Middle East Shi'ites may feel in their home countries because of unfair political and economic treatment. U.S. leadership correspondingly needs to recognize that while this may be the wrong time to push for full democracy in the larger Middle East, it is the right time to push for reform including the acceptable treatment of Shi'ite citizens by Arab countries. Reducing or eliminating discrimination against Shi'ites in Sunni Arab countries is an important component of any strategy to contain sectarian spill-over.

2. The United States needs to consider carefully the dangers that sectarian disorder may bring to Iraq's neighbors, even in the case of those countries which are U.S. adversaries. If Syria collapses into chaos, this development will not serve U.S. interests. A decrepit Ba'ath regime, however unpleasant and troublesome, is a better option for the present than a Syrian civil war or the extreme and energized Islamist regime that could emerge from such chaos. Ba'athism in Syria, in general, may not have much of a future. At this time, it is probably most useful to take advantage of Syrian isolation and weakness to seek continuing gains in Syrian behavior towards Iraq.

3. The United States needs to let its Iraqi friends and allies know that they will be welcomed into the United States should they face disaster in Iraq rather than consigned to be refugees in some other part of the world. Such policies do not mean that we are facing and preparing for defeat in Iraq. Rather, they would be meant to reassure our Iraqi supporters that we will stand by them regardless of the problems that they might face. Like all forms of insurance, this approach is meant to be comforting and empowering to our Iraqi supporters. The United States should also continue and expand programs to allow actively pro-American Iraqis and their families into the United States and then allow the heads of household to return to Iraq to work with U.S. forces if they are willing and can make a useful contribution to building the new Iraq. The U.S. willingness to protect the families of such supporters in this way builds good will and enhances U.S. ability to recruit especially valuable supporters. While many such families would have permanent resident status, they would probably be interested in returning to Iraq once they felt safe in doing so.

4. The U.S. leadership needs to understand that foreign terrorists and funds may return to Iraq after being driven out unless Sunni tribal groups in Western Iraq can maintain good relations with each other and good relations with the Baghdad government. The Awakening groups therefore cannot be precipitously abolished thereby repeating the same type of mistake as disbanding the Iraqi Army in 2003. Zero-sum thinking on the part of key Iraqi leaders could lead to intersectarian and intrasectarian problems that plunge Western Iraq into renewed chaos. If Iraqi leaders are determined to seek political advantages by plunging the country into a downward cycle, U.S. forces will be able to do very little about it. Terrorist infiltration from abroad would again become a larger problem, and the danger presented to the region by Iraq trained terrorists would be increased.

5. The United States needs to take whatever steps are necessary to minimize the ability of al-Qaeda members to infiltrate Iraq at any future point, but especially at the beginning of that stage where the Iraqi government is seeking to survive and expand its authority following the eventual departure of U.S.

troops. This program to help Iraq may involve limited cooperation with Syria and under some circumstances, Iran. Such cooperation should be limited but could also be used to set the stage for a discussion of other problems including nuclear weapons in Iran and problems with support for terrorist groups by both countries.

6. The United States must do all it can to maintain intelligence data bases that reflect the movements of foreign fighters who have left Iraq after gaining valuable experience there and must keep this need in mind when developing policies toward all Arab countries including Syria. In this regard, it is again doubtful that either U.S. or Israeli interests would be well served by regime change in Damascus that led to an almost totally anarchic situation such as that found in Iraq as late as 2006. Intelligence cooperation with the Syrians should be considered if the Syrian regime is willing to provide useful intelligence on an ongoing basis, and if the price that the Syrians want for such cooperation is not unacceptably high.

7. The United States needs to be aware that al-Qaeda has very little to offer the Arab world except what they seek to present as a heroic image, which they seek to enhance through fighting Western and especially U.S. troops. Moreover, when al-Qaeda's violent tendencies cause it to kill innocent Arab civilians, as it did in Jordan in November 2005, it pays a massive price in public sympathy, and tends to be met with strong state resistance. It is therefore almost always better to have responsible Arab forces fighting al-Qaeda whenever this is possible, even if they are often not as effective as U.S. forces. Efforts by Arab countries such as Jordan to provide counterterrorism support to fellow Arab states should be encouraged and supported financially by the United States on a continuing basis throughout the struggle against terrorism.

8. U.S. leaders will have to consider and prepare for the possibility that organized crime based in Iraq could grow and become more transnational over time. While narcotics smuggling may become a more serious problem at a later point, one of the most immediate issues may become weapons trafficking. This problem will be difficult to control, although there are numerous measures for weapons accountability that would seem possible should Iraq be able to move itself to ever increasing levels of stability. Everything must also be done to prevent the drug trade from becoming an entrenched part of the Iraqi political system. Various regional, tribal, and militia leaders will always be interested in money-making enterprises that can help them finance an independent power base. Corrupt officials involved in such practices will need to be prosecuted by the Iraqi government to the fullest extent. The United States will also need to support efforts to prosecute corrupt Iraqis for international crimes that reach beyond Iraqi borders.

9. The United States needs to keep seeking ways to support Iraqi unity. A calm Iraq subdued by the U.S. military and its allies should not be mistaken for a united Iraq. An Iraq where all of the regions benefit by cooperation with the central government is especially important. In this regard, the return of international oil companies to Iraq will only have a useful influence on that country if this is handled in a well-planned way that does not encourage or support Kurdish separatism or Sunni-Shi'ite strife. Likewise, no future U.S.-Iraqi security arrangements, including basing, should be done in such a way as to appear to encourage Kurdish separatism.

10. The United States needs to continue and expand its coordination with Iraq's Arab neighbors on addressing Iraq-related issues. There have been only limited results with such coordination in the past, but there are important signs this situation might improve. Many of Iraq's neighbors, including Jordan, Saudi Arabia, Bahrain and Kuwait, now maintain or have agreed to establish full diplomatic relations with Iraq. As neighboring states become increasingly aware of the U.S. intention to reduce its troop presence in Iraq, the national interests of all neighboring states may press them towards a set of policies that accept the new Iraqi government even if they remain unhappy that it is Shi'ite dominated and that it was enabled by a U.S.-led invasion. A key problem here will be to avoid a scenario whereby Sunni Arab states are supporting Sunni maximalists in Iraq while the Iranians are supporting radical Shi'ite maximalists there. At some point, it may be necessary for Iraq's neighbors to work together to back away from such dangers provided that the political will for these efforts exists in all of the countries involved. This will be difficult with Iran under the present leadership, but it may not be hopeless provided the Iranians are willing to scale back at least some of their activities in Iraq provided Saudi Arabia does the same.

ENDNOTES

1. Karen DeYoung, "U.S., Iraq Scale Down Negotiations Over Forces," *Washington Post*, July 13, 2008, p. 1; Sudarsan Raghavan, "Iraqis Differ on Obama's Plans," *Washington Post*, July 19, 2008, p. 7; Robert Burns, "U.S. Has Mixed Feelings About Iraqi Confidence," *San Diego Union Tribune*, July 14, 2008, internet.

2. See Joshua Partlow, "U.S. Strategy on Sunnis Questioned," *Washington Post*, June 18, 2007, p. A11.

3. John Hatch, *The History of Britain in Africa: From the Fifteenth Century to the Present*, New York: Praeger, 1969, Chapter 10; Jon Woronoff, *Organizing African Unity*, Metuchen, NJ: Scarecrow Press, 1970, p. 120.

4. International Crisis Group (ICG), *Failed Responsibility: Iraqi Refugees in Syria, Jordan, and Lebanon*, Brussels, Belgium: International Crisis Group, July 2008, p. 1.

5. Ali A. Allawi, *The Occupation of Iraq: Winning the War, Losing the Peace*, New Haven and London: Yale University Press, 2007, p. 123.

6. Office of the United Nations High Commissioner for Refugees (UNHCR), "Statistics of Displaced Iraqis Around the World," September 2007, internet.

7. Patrick Cockburn, *Muqtada: Muqtada al Sadr, the Shia Revival and the Struggle for Iraq*, New York: Scribner, 2008, p. 68.

8. Lyse Doucet, "Refugees Create New 'Baghdad'," *BBC News*, April 21, 2007, internet.

9. Gina Chon, "Iraq, 5 Years On, A Nation of Refugees," *Wall Street Journal*, March 17, 2008, p. 1.

10. "Iraq and the Kurds: A Truly National Army," *Economist*, May 19, 2007, p. 54.

11. "Forced Displacement Takes Heavy Toll on Families," *Jordan Times*, March 17, 2008, internet.

12. International Crisis Group, *Iraq's Civil War, The Sadrists and the Surge*, Brussels, Belgium, February 2008, p. 7.

13. Cockburn, *Muqtada,* p. 84.

14. Central Intelligence Agency (CIA), *World Factbook*, Washington, DC: U.S. Government Printing Office, 2008, internet.

15. Sally Buzbee, "Iraq Strives for Growth in Jobs," *Boston Globe*, July 18, 2008, internet.

16. Damien Cave, "Nonstop Theft and Bribery are Staggering Iraq," *New York Times*, December 2, 2007, p. 1.

17. Tina Susman and Raheem Salman, "Iraq's Middle Class is Languishing," *Los Angeles Times*, January 6, 2008, internet.

18. Sam Dagher, "Iraqis More Secure, But Few are Finding Jobs," *Christian Science Monitor*, July 28, 2008, p. 1.

19. John F. Burns, "Jordan's King, In Gamble, Lends Hand to the U.S.," *New York Times*, March 3, 2003, internet.

20. Cockburn, p. 92.

21. Ben Sanders and Merrill Smith, "The Iraqi Refugee Disaster," *World Policy Journal*, Fall 2007, p. 26.

22. Sameer N. Yacoub, "Iraq Says Doctors Can Carry Guns for Protection," *Washington Post*, September 29, 2008, internet.

23. Robin Wright, *Dreams and Shadows: The Future of the Middle East*, New York: Penguin Press, 2008, p. 412. Some sources claim this practice has been discontinued, although the situation remains unclear.

24. Many Iraqi refugees, including children, have witnessed unspeakable acts of murder, torture, and other crimes and are consequently in potential need of mental health services. See Linda Hindi, "50% of Displaced Iraqis Need Psycho-Social Support—Reports," *Jordan Times*, April 7, 2008, internet.

25. Allawi, p. 128.

26. Bassem Mroue, "Syria bars Iraq refugees, Crisis Worsens," *Washington Post*, February 12, 2007, internet.

27. As recently as May 2008, the author met numerous average people in Jordan who are convinced that their economic situation has declined because of the spending habits of Iraqi refugees in Amman.

28. Deborah Campbell, "Exodus: Where Will Iraq Go Next?" *Harper's Magazine*, April 2008, p. 54.

29. Constant Brand, "EU Ready to Take Up to 10,000 More Iraqi Refugees," *Washington Post*, September 25, 2008, internet.

30. Mary Jordan, "Iraqi Refugees Find Sweden's Doors Closing," *Washington Post*, April 10, 2008, internet.

31. Ben Sanders and Merrill Smith, "The Iraqi Refugee Disaster," *World Policy Journal*, Fall 2007, p. 23.

32. "U.S. Exceeds Goal in Admitting Iraqis," *Washington Times*, October 2, 2008, p. 2.

33. Alissa J. Rubin, "U.S. Expands VISA Program for Iraqis," *New York Times*, July 25, 2008, internet.

34. Linda Hindi, "Jordan to Host Iraq Refugees Meeting," *Jordan Times*, March 17, 2008, internet.

35. ICG, *Failed Responsibility*, p. 5.

36. Sanders and Smith, p. 26.

37. Alessa J. Rubin, "Shiite Refugees Feel Forsaken in Their Holy City," *New York Times*, October 19, 2007, p. 1.

38. Government Accountability Office, *Securing, Stabilizing and Rebuilding Iraq: Progress Report: Some Gains Made, Updated Strategy Needed*, Washington DC: U.S. GAO, June 2008, p. 16.

39. Campbell, p. 56.

40. "Iraqis in Syria Hike Prices, Overcrowd Schools," *Jordan Times*, February 22, 2007, internet.

41. ICG, *Failed Responsibility*, p. 16.

42. "U.S. Officials Holds Talks on Refugees," *Washington Times*, June 25, 2008, p. 20.

43. "Iraqis in Syria Hike Prices, Overcrowd Schools," *Jordan Times*.

44. Campbell, *Exodus*, p. 56.

45. *Ibid.*, p. 52.

46. ICG, *Failed Responsibility*, p. 20.

47. Nikolaos Van Dam, *The Struggle for Power in Syria: Politics and Society Under Asad and the Ba'ath Party*, London: I. B. Tauris, 1996, chapters 7 and 8.

48. *Ibid*, p. 20.

49. Campbell, *Exodus*, p. 52.

50. *Ibid.*, p. 56.

51. Sabrina Tavernise, "Jordan Yields Poverty and Pain for the Well-Off Fleeing Iraq," *New York Times*, August 10, 2007, internet.

52. *Ibid.*

53. Hindi, "Jordan to host Iraq Refugees Meeting."

54. Linda Hindi, "Iraqi Expatriates Around Half a Million," *Jordan Times*, November 14, 2007, internet.

55. Linda Hindi, "Iraqis Welcome Decision on Fines, but Question Impact," *Jordan Times*, February 15, 2008, internet.

56. On the price of oil after the war, see Sana Abdullah, "Jordan: Appeasing the Tribes," *Middle East International*, July 22, 2005, p. 16.

57. Omar Fekeiki and Yasmine Mousa, "Living in Jordan, Longing for Iraq," *Washington Post*, August 5, 2006, p. A15.

58. Tom A. Peter, "Iraqi Refugees Spill into Jordan, Driving Up Prices," *Christian Science Monitor*, November 29, 2006, internet.

59. Ibrahim Saif and David M. DeBartolo, *The Iraq War's Impact on Growth and Inflation in Jordan*, Amman, Jordan: Center for Strategic Studies, University of Jordan, 2007, especially pp. 38-40.

60. See Sana Abdallah, "Jordan: Row with Iraq," *Middle East International*, April 1, 2005, pp. 14-15. Also note that the number of Shi'ite refugees in Jordan is extremely difficult to establish. It is possible that some Shi'ites are representing themselves as Sunnis in the belief that they will thereby be better received in Jordan.

61. David Enders, "A Million Iraqis Flee War-Torn Country for Haven in Jordan," *Washington Times*, May 27, 2006, p. 6.

62. "Jordan Tightens Iraqi Immigration," *BBC News*, February 28, 2007, internet.

63. "Egypt: Respond to the Needs of Iraqi Refugees," April 12, 2007, as cited by *refugeesinternational.org*, internet.

64. "UNHCR Hails Decision by Beirut to Legalize Iraqi Refugees as Positive," *Daily Star*, February 22, 2008, internet.

65. "Lebanon a Tough Place for Iraqi Refugees," *Kuwait Times*, December 17, 2007, internet.

66. "Palestinians in Lebanon: A History of the Hapless," *Economist*, June 2, 2007, p. 46.

67. Campbell, p. 53.

68. Associated Press, "U.N. Refugee Body Criticizes Turkey for Forcefully Returning Refugees," *International Herald Tribune*, July 26, 2007, internet.

69. "Kuwaitis Still Oppose Reopening Ties with Iraq," *Kuwait Times*, August 3, 2008, internet.

70. Author's interviews with senior Kuwaiti civilian and military officials, Kuwait City, April 2007.

71. Alexandra Zavis, "U.N. Plans to Aid Iraqi Refugees," *Los Angeles Times*, December 5, 2007, internet.

72. James Warden, "Shiites' Return to Dora Sparks Tensions, Blasts," *Mideast Stars and Stripes*, March 15, 2008, internet.

73. Tim Susman, "Some Iraqi Returnees Face Uncertain Lives," *Los Angeles Times*, December 13, 2007, internet.

74. See Major Niel Smith and Colonel Sean MacFarland, "Anbar Awakens: The Tipping Point," *Military Review*, March-April 2008, pp. 21-52.

75. "Interview with General David Petraeus, 'The Reality is Very Hard'," *Newsweek*, January 14, 2008, internet.

76. International Crisis Group, *Iraq after the Surge I: The New Landscape*, Brussels, Belgium: ICG, April 30, 2008, pp. 5-9.

77. David Kilcullen as quoted in ICG, *Iraq After the Surge I*, p. 14.

78. The Arabic translation of "Concerned Local Citizens" was something like worried residents and was therefore replaced with the more martial "Sons of Iraq" designation.

79. AFP, "At Least 44 Die on Day US and Iraq Start Talks on Future ties," *Daily Star*, March 12, 2008, internet.

80. Babak Dehghanpisheh and Evan Thomas, "Scions of the Surge," *Newsweek*, March 23, 2008, p. 32.

81. Erica Goode, "Friction Infiltrates Sunni Patrols on Safer Iraqi Streets," *New York Times*, September 23, 2008, internet; Ernesto Londono, "For U.S. and Sunni Allies, A Turning Point," *Washington Post*, September 30, 2008, internet.

82. Sudarsan Raghavan, "New Leaders of Sunnis Make Gains in Influence," *Washington Post*, January 8, 2008, p. 1.

83. Solomon Moore, "Ex-Baathists get a break. Or do They," *New York Times*, January 14, 2008, p. 6.

84. "Iraq: Wobbling all over the place," *Economist*, March 29, 2008, p. 59.

85. Jim Michaels, "Foreign Fighters Getting Out of Iraq, Military Says," *USA Today*, March 21, 2008, p. 6.

86. "Top Qaeda Figure Nabbed," *Kuwait Times*, July 18, 2007, internet.

87. ICG, *Iraq After the Surge I*, p. 21; Tom A. Peter, "Iraqi Insurgents Forced Underground," *Christian Science Monitor*, September 23, 2008, p. 1.

88. Associated Press, "Emboldened Iraqi Tipsters Reveal More Weapons Caches," *Arizona Daily Star*, June 20, 2008, internet.

89. "Teens Trained to be bombers," *Bahrain Tribune*, May 27, 2008, internet.

90. Rowan Scarborough, "U.S. Military's Restraint Not al-Qaeda's War Code," *Washington Times*, February 12, 2008, p. 3; Steven R. Hurst, "Blast Shows Tenacity of al-Qaeda in Iraq," *Philadelphia Inquirer*, February 12, 2008, internet; Borzou Daragahi, "Iraqi Neighborhood Mourns Dead After Bombings," *Los Angeles Times*, March 8, 2008, internet.

91. GAO, *Securing and Stabilizing and Rebuilding Iraq*, p. 31.

92. Anthony H. Cordesman, "Iraq and Foreign Volunteers: Working Draft," Washington DC: Center for Strategic and International Studies, November 18, 2005, pp. 1-9. Note that this short study has some interesting information on Saudi Arabian radicals in Iraq.

93. "Declassified Key Judgments of the National Intelligence Estimate, *Trends in Global Terrorism: Implications for the United States*, dated April 2006," as cited in Director of National Intelligence Press Release, September 26, 2006, internet. This danger has been commented upon with concern by the former head of the CIA's bin Laden unit, Michael Scheuer. See Michael Scheuer, *Marching Toward Hell: America and the Islam After Iraq*, New York: Free Press, 2008, Chapter 4.

94. "Al-Qaeda in Retreat—CIA Chief," BBC News, May 30, 2008, internet.

95. These concerns have been aggravated by high profile scandals such as the Abu Gharib prison abuse disaster and pan-Arab news coverage that is unfriendly to the U.S. presence in Iraq.

96. Lawrence, p. 179.

97. Jim Michaels, "Foreign Fighters Getting Out of Iraq, Military Says," USA Today, March 21, 2008, p. 6.

98. This tactic can result in casualties to the force that captured the prisoner, although the terrorist is virtually always killed. Lawrence, p. 181.

99. Joseph Felter and Brian Fishman, Al-Qa'ida's Foreign Fighters in Iraq: A First Look at the Sinjar Records, West Point, New York: Combating Terrorism Center, 2008, p. 16. Note the Sinjar records were captured by coalition forces in an October 2007 raid.

100. Marie Colvin, "Iraqis Lead Final Purge of al-Qaeda," London Sunday Times, July 6, 2008, internet.

101. "Kuwaiti Citizen Arrested for recruiting jihadists," Kuwait Times, July 11, 2008, internet; Associated Press, "More Foreign Militants Operating in Pakistan, Joint Chiefs' Boss Says," San Diego Union-Tribune, July 11, 2008, internet. Also see Albert Aji, "Syria Displays New Iraq Border Security," Washington Post, November 10, 2007, internet.

102. "Syria Boosts Security along Iraq Border," USA Today, October 28, 2005, internet.

103. "Fewer Thugs Entering Iraq," Reuters, February 12, 2008, internet.

104. Associated Press, "Al-Qaeda Turns More to Extortion, Abduction to Fund Fight, U.S. Says," San Diego Union-Tribune,

July 28, 2008, internet; "Iraqi Militants 'raising' money through crime," *Kuwait Times*, July 31, 2008, internet.

105. Jean-Charles Brisard, *Zarqawi: The New Face of Al-Qaeda*, New York: Other Press, 2005, Chapter 5.

106. *Ibid.*, pp. 28-29.

107. On the concept of far and near enemies, see Gilles Kepel, *The War for Muslim Minds: Islam and the West*, Cambridge, MA, and London: The Belknap Press of Harvard University Press, 2004, Chapter 3.

108. The 1980s movie *Rambo II,* in which a muscular American hero fights beside the Afghans against the Soviets, is still enormously popular in Afghanistan.

109. "Targeting Innocents," *The Middle East*, December 2005, p. 15.

110. Wright, p. 5.

111. According to the Pew Global Attitudes public opinion survey, sympathy for al-Qaeda was at 20 percent in 2007, down from 56 percent in 2002. See "Reassuring, But Not Surprising," *Jordan Times*, September 28, 2007, internet.

112. Alan George, *Jordan: Living in the Crossfire*, London and New York: Zed Books, 2005, p. 62.

113. The author has dealt with this topic in W. Andrew Terrill, *Jordanian National Security and the Future of Middle East Stability*, Carlisle, PA: Strategic Studies Institute, U.S. Army War College, 2008, pp. 44-46.

114. *Ibid.*, pp. 44-46.

115. Norton, p. 438.

116. "3 Killed in Lebanon Refugee Camp Brawl," *Kuwait Times*, July 21, 2008, internet.

117. Norton, p. 438.

118. Rami J. Khouri, "Middle East Conflicts Converge in North Lebanon Fighting," *Jordan Times*, May 25-26, 2007, internet.

119. "Iraq 'Exporting' Islamist Fighters," *Kuwait Times*, May 29, 2007, internet.

120. Reuters, "US Sees Signs of al-Qaeda in Yemen Attacks," *Khaleej Times*, September 18, 2008, internet.

121. For a comprehensive and towering 1,283-page work on Iraqi history and factionalism, see Hanna Batatu, *The Old Social Classes and the Revolutionary Movements of Iraq*, London: Saqi Books, 2004.

122. Allawi, p. 132.

123. *Ibid.*, p 127.

124. Thomas P. Odom, *Journey into Darkness: Genocide in Rwanda*, College Station: Texas A&M Press, 2005, p. 165.

125. See Sabrina Tavernise, "Relations Sour Between Shiites and Iraq Militia," *New York Times*, October 12, 2007, p. 1.

126. The January 2005 election involved a Sunni Arab boycott of the polls out of conviction in some cases and because of terrorist threats in other cases. The tactic backfired, however, and Sunni Arab turnout was impressive in subsequent elections. See Allawi, pp. 389-390.

127. International Crisis Group, *The Next Iraqi War? Sectarianism and Civil Conflict*, Brussels, Belgium: ICG, February 2006, p. 29.

128. Zarqawi as cited in Augustus Richard Norton, "The Shiite 'Threat' Revisited," *Current History*, December 2007, p. 437.

129. Sadr also had problems because the Iranians intervened politically on Maliki's behalf during the fighting in Basra. See Ned Parker, "Iraq's Nouri Maliki Breaking Free of U.S.," *Los Angeles Times*, September 16, 2008, internet.

130. Alexandra Zavis, "In Iraq, Role of Tribes is Divisive," *Los Angeles Times*, June 23, 2007, p. 1.

131. The last ruling Shi'ite dynasty in the Arab World was the Fatimids of Egypt who were overthrown by the great Sunni Muslim leader, Saladin, in 1171.

132. Campbell, p. 51.

133. Yitzhak Nakash, *Reaching for Power, The Shi'a in the Modern Arab World*, Princeton and Oxford: Princeton University Press, 2006, p. 50.

134. See Toby Jones, "Saudi Arabia's Not So New Anti-Shi'sim," *Middle East Report*, Spring 2007, pp. 29-32; "Saudi Shiite Held after Meeting King," *Kuwait Times*, May 19, 2008, internet.

135. Lori Plotkin Boghardt, *Kuwait Amid War, Peace and Revolution 1979-1991*, New York: Palgrave MacMillan, 2006, pp. 110-119.

136. Morten Valbjorn and Andre Bank, "Signs of a New Arab Cold War: The 2006 Lebanon War and the Sunni-Shi'i Divide," *Middle East Report*, Spring 2007, pp. 6-11.

137. Zaki Chehab, *Inside Hamas: The Untold Story of the Militant Islamic Movement*, New York: Nation Books, 2007, pp. 134-143; Shaul Mishal and Aviaham Sela, *The Palestinian Hamas, Vision, Violence, and Coexistence*, New York: Columbia University Press, 2000, p. 97.

138. Agence France Presse, "Iraq's Neighbours Pledge to Help Fight Insurgency," *Gulf in the Media*, October 24, 2007, internet.

139. Ed Blanche, "Shifting Sands," *The Middle East*, January 2008, pp. 16-17.

140. B. Izzak, "Expat Mughniyah Mourners To Be Deported," *Kuwait Times*, March 3, 2008, internet.

141. Argentine authorities issued an arrest warrant for Mughniyah in conjunction with the 1980s bombing of the Israeli embassy in Buenos Aries, killing 29 people. See Augustus Richard Norton, *Hizbollah: A Short History*, Princeton and Oxford: Princeton University Press, 2007, p. 79.

142. "Kuwaiti Lawyers Sue Shiite MPs Over Slain Hezballah Commander," Kuwait News Agency, February 21, 2008, internet.

143. B. Izzak, "Expat Mughniyah Mourners to be Deported," *Kuwait Times*, March 3, 2008, internet.

144. *Ibid.*

145. "Shia Crackdown Sparks Sectarian Tension in Kuwait," Agence France-Presse, March 14, 2008, internet.

146. Christopher Davidson, "Sunni-Shiite Hostility: The UAE Suggests Otherwise," *Daily Star*, August 4, 2008, internet.

147. "Kurds Hoist Reworked Iraqi Flag," *BBC News*, February 10, 2008, internet.

148. Quil Lawrence, *Invisible Nation: How the Kurds' Quest for Statehood is Shaping Iraq and the Middle East*, New York: Walker & Company, 2008, p. 137.

149. Ned Parker, "Ruling Partners Pressure Iraq Premier," *Los Angeles Times*, February 8, 2008, internet.

150. Associated Press, "Iraq Moves to Break up Kurds' Oil Deals," *San Diego Union Tribune*, January 18, 2008, internet.

151. "Baghdad, Kurdish North Forms Panel to Discuss Oil," *Daily Star* (Beirut), June 30, 2008, internet.

152. Lawrence, p. 186; Ned Parker, "A Battle for Land in Northern Iraq," *Los Angeles Times*, April 5, 2008, p. 1.

153. George Packer, *The Assassin's Gate: America in Iraq*, New York: Farrar, Straus, and Giroux, 2005, p. 342.

154. Alissa J. Rubin and Sabrina Tavernise, "Turkish Planes Strike Iraqi Kurdistan," *New York Times*, February 5, 2008, internet.

155. Human Rights Watch, *Claims in Conflict: Reversing Ethnic Cleansing in Northern Iraq*, August 2004, Section III, internet; George Packer, "The Next Iraqi War?" *The New Yorker*, October 4, 2004, p. 68.

156. Jeffrey Goldberg, "After Iraq," *The Atlantic*, January/February 2008, p. 79.

157. Lawrence, p. 186.

158. *Ibid.*, p. 185. Also note that while the PKK has officially changed its name to Kongra Gel, it is still almost universally known as the PKK.

159. The author has traveled to Turkey on numerous occasions since 1992, especially in the last few years.

160. Umit Enginsoy, "Iraqi Kurds Have Territorial Ambitions on Turkey, Top Diplomat Implies," *Turkish Daily News*, July 13, 2007, internet.

161. William Hale, *Turkey, the US and Iraq*, London: SAQI Publishers, 2007, pp. 76-77.

162. Lawrence, p. 190.

163. "Turkish Troops Enter Iraq," *The Times*, February 23, 2008, p. 1; Joshua Partlow, "A Kurdish Society of Soldiers," *Washington Post*, March 8, 2008, p. 1.

164. Lawrence, p. 151.

165. *Ibid.*, p. 148.

166. Some Kurdish forces claim strikes have occurred since 2004.

167. Ed Blanche, "Kurdish Powder Keg," *The Middle East*, January 2008, p. 27.

168. "Report: Iran Official Says Iran Shelled Kurds," *USA Today*, September 25, 2007, internet.

169. Ahmed S. Hashim, *Insurgency and Counter-Insurgency*, Ithaca, NY: Cornell University Press, 2006, p. 170.

170. See Phil Williams, "Organized Crime and Corruption in Iraq," forthcoming, in *International Peacekeeping*; and Mark Hozenball, "Iraq's Black Gold," *Newsweek*, November 11, 2002, p. 27.

171. *Ibid.*

172. Allawi, pp. 122-123.

173. United Nations Office on Drugs and Crime, *Addressing Organized Crime and Drug Trafficking in Iraq: Report of the UNODC Fact Finding Mission*, August 15-18, 2003, UNODC: Vienna, August 25, 2003, p. 4.

174. Allawi, p. 169.

175. Cockburn, p. 115.

176. Anthony Shadid, *Night Draws Near: Iraq's People in the Shadow of America' War*, New York: Henry Hold and Company, 2005, p. 134.

177. Allawi, p. 126.

178. Iraqi scholar Mustafa Alani, as cited in "Kuwaiti, Iraqi and European Perspectives," *Middle East Policy*, Fall 2004, internet.

179. Bruce R. Pirnie and Edward O'Connell, *Counterinsurgency in Iraq (2003-2006)*, Santa Monica, CA, and Washington, DC: RAND Corporation, 2008, p. 49.

180. Ali A. Allawi, *The Occupation of Iraq: Winning the War, Losing the Peace*, New Haven and London: Yale University Press, 2007, p. 118.

181. Iraq officials interviewed by the author seldom deny the existence of crime and corruption, but rather attempt to explain that poor salaries and crushing poverty make it a natural phenomenon.

182. Sabrina Tavernise, "Relations Sour Between Shiites and Iraq Militias," *New York Times*, October 12, 2007, p. 1.

183. "Iraq: The Enigma of Muqtada al-Sadr," *The Economist*, February 16, 2008, pp. 53-54.

184. James A. Baker III and Lee H. Hamilton, (co-chairs) *The Iraq Study Group Report*, New York: Vintage Books, 2006, p. 29.

185. Glenn Kessler, "Weapons Given to Iraq Are Missing," *Washington Post*, August 6, 2007, p. 1.

186. Thomas Land, "Drug Trade Takes Its Toll in Middle East Region," *The Middle East*, June 2008, p. 21.

187. Thomas Schweich, "Is Afghanistan a Narco-State?" *The New York Times Magazine*, July 27, 2008, internet; "Karzai: Eyes Wide Shut on Drugs," *Bahrain Tribune*, July 25, 2008, internet.

188. A. Saleh, "Court Upholds Death for Royals," *Kuwait Times*, December 11, 2007, internet.

189. Sabrina Tavernise, "Violence Leaves Young Iraqis Doubting Clerics," *New York Times*, March 4, 2008, p. 1.